The Story of Modern Protestant Theology

The Story of Modern Protestant Theology

Klaus Bockmuehl

REGENT COLLEGE PUBLISHING
Vancouver, British Columbia

The Story of Modern Protestant Theology
Copyright © 2007 Elisabeth Bockmuehl

All rights reserved. No part of this publication may be reproduced, stored in a retrieval system, or transmitted, in any form or by any means, electronic, mechanical, photocopying, recording or otherwise, without the prior written permission of the author, except in the case of brief quotations embodied in critical articles and reviews.

Published 2007 by Regent College Publishing
5800 University Boulevard, Vancouver, BC V6T 2E4 Canada
Web: www.regentpublishing.com
E-mail: info@regentpublishing.com

Regent College Publishing is an imprint of the Regent Bookstore <www.regentbookstore.com>. Views expressed in works published by Regent College Publishing are those of the author and do not necessarily represent the official position of Regent College <www.regent-college.edu>.

Book design by Robert Hand
<roberthandcommunications.com>

Library and Archives Canada Cataloguing in Publication Data

Bockmuehl, Klaus, 1931–1989
  The story of Protestant theology / Klaus Bockmuehl.

Based on lectures given at Regent College in the mid-1980s.
Includes bibliographical references.
ISBN 1–57383–337–1

1. Protestant churches—Doctrines. I. Title.

BT80.B62 2007   230'.044   C2006-906248-X

CONTENTS

	Editors' Foreword	ix
	Introduction	xi
1.	Friedrich Daniel Ernst Schleiermacher (1768–1834)	19
2.	Liberalism Within the Church: Albrecht Ritschl (1822–1829)	67
3.	The Post-Ritschl Liberal School	87
4.	The Evangelical Alternative	99
5.	Karl Barth (1886–1968)	125
6.	Emil Brunner (1889–1966)	187
7.	Rudolf Bultmann (1884–1976)	219
8.	Current Issues and Figures in Theology	243

"*When the Bible is ransacked like this, it is no wonder that salvation becomes merely a modest program for self-improvement.*"

Editors' Foreword

"When the Bible is ransacked like this, it is no wonder that salvation becomes merely a modest program for self-improvement." This statement, taken from the text that follows (58), is at once both critical and provocative. Does the entire tradition of "liberal theology" from Friedrich Schleiermacher forward indeed amount to little more than a theological version of self-help psychology? Is Ludwig Feuerbach the inevitable result of such an enterprise? If so, should the blame indeed be laid at the door of modern critical biblical scholarship, as the opening quotation might suggest? It goes without saying that not all will be able to answer in the affirmative to these questions, but then again, Klaus Bockmuehl would not have expected anything else.

To the contrary. Those who knew him will be the first to attest to his quick wit and capacity for learned critique. He was a capable scholar who made informed indictments against those with whom he disagreed. In the same breath, however, those who knew him will also hasten to note that theology, for Bockmuehl, was not simply an exercise in gratuitous polemics. It was, for him, a form of *spirituality*—an exercise undertaken in prayer, for the church. One hears echoes of Karl Barth.

Whether or not the reader agrees with Bockmuehl on every point, surely this theolgical-devotional impulse is one that we would all do well to heed. For this reason, one

Editors' Foreword

of Bockmuehl's own brief meditations on a passage from the Psalms will be found before each chapter. Because each chapter is a modified form of lectures given over the course of his career, and because it was Bockmuehl's custom to begin each class period with such a meditation, we felt it both appropriate and expedient to include them in the final product. It is hoped that their inclusion will serve as a constant reminder that the dialectics of theological argument are most profitably undertaken in the context of the dialectics of prayer and meditation. Martin Luther would not have it any other way.

The lectures that serve as the basis for this book were given in a graduate course in modern Protestant theology at Regent College, Vancouver, where Bockmuehl taught theology until his death in 1989. The oral nature of the material intentionally has been retained. Because the material was given originally in lecture format, references to original sources have not been recorded.

The book in its present form would not have been possible without the help of numerous people over the years. Mark Buchanan, Jonathan Mills, Pete Santucci, Rob Clements, Robert Hand and Bill Reimer all, at various points and in various ways, have contributed to its final form. Collectively, we can only hope that the lively, prayerful spirit of Klaus Bockmuehl will be preserved in what follows for generations yet to come.

Vancouver, 2007

Introduction

THE BIBLICAL MESSAGE AND ITS CONEXTUALIZATION

The work of theology is governed by two concerns. The first is the continuous need to translate the biblical message afresh for each new generation. The second is the need to accomplish this translation without loss of biblical substance. The first task is similar to what missionaries must do in cross-cultural missions: just as missionaries must adapt the message to new cultural and geographical settings, so theologians must adapt the message for new eras. In both cases, the task of translation can be called "contextualization" or, to use a less fortunate term, "enculturation." The importance of hermeneutics lies here. Hermeneutics is the enterprise of translating the biblical message not simply into a culture's language, but into that culture's thought forms, its images and idioms, its dialect. Such work must range over both time and space, geography and generation. Just as the world and worldview of a laundryman in Calcutta is different from that of a businesswoman in Manhattan today, so also across history people's thought patterns, the formative experiences, the familiar images, the ways of seeing and knowing, differ from generation to generation, sometimes even from decade to decade. Contextualization seeks to bridge these distances. It is the art of adaptation, of keeping the ancient message from becoming merely archaic words. It must ensure that the old remains new, so that words uttered or written thousands of years past continue to speak with force and vitality in the present.

It is difficult to understand the theologians, the orthodox Reformed ones, for example, who believe that everything that was necessary and worth saying was said and published before 1700. According to such theologians, the only thing left to do is to reprint the old books. For them there is no need to struggle in order to explain the gospel to our own generation. Theirs is a stance of mere traditionalism. Admittedly, traditionalism is rooted in a legitimate fear, since it seeks to safeguard the Gospel from distortion and dilution. So it is here that the second concern of theology comes into play: contextualization must be exercised without loss of the original biblical material. Continuity with the genuine biblical message must be maintained in the process of translation. The biblical message might be fitted into thought forms which are defective and be deformed or diminished this way, like a body forced into a shrunken or ill-tailored suit. Theology, therefore, is the art of avoiding these extremes, between deadness on the one hand and dissolution on the other. At one extreme is an accommodation to culture so thorough that Christianity is subsumed into culture. That is always the fate of "culture Christianity": the Gospel vanishes without trace and only culture remains. At the other extreme is a kind of counter-culture Christianity—a withdrawal into a ghetto closed off from the larger society. Such Christianity refuses to do the job of translating the Gospel for the surrounding culture. It may maintain its purity (though that is debatable) but at the cost of witness. There are, of course, a variety of stances between these two extremes, but the test of theology is how

Introduction

well it has solved this two-fold task, how well it has forged a message which retains basic biblical content while reaching out to the surrounding culture. Theology must show us how to engage culture without succumbing to culture.

GOD'S SOVEREIGNTY AND THE CULTURE OF SECULAR HUMANISM

In our survey of the theology of the nineteenth and twentieth centuries, we will encounter the different theological forms that this two-fold task has generated. The problem is the same for each generation. But for the last 150 years, the problem has acquired some new and thorny dilemmas. For in that time in the West, the encounter between the Gospel and culture has been an encounter between the Christian message and secular humanism—a culture that rejects the doctrine of Divine sovereignty.

Modern theology is conducted in the shadow of the Enlightenment. (The Enlightenment, though usually said to begin in the late eighteenth century, actually has its roots in the Italian Renaissance.) Enlightenment philosophy represents in extreme form the postulate of man's autonomy and omnipotence. Since the Enlightenment period when this philosophy began to seep into the mainstream of Western thought, theology has had to cope with secular humanism and its dictates—both philosophic and moral. The task for theology in this encounter is enormous, for theology is required to interpret the content of the Christian message into thought categories which have been colored and shaped by secular humanism. It is a task almost like trying to capture fire in paper bags: the container is unfit for the contents. Nevertheless, the attempt must be made. Friedrich Schleiermacher's first book, *On Religion: Speeches to Its Cultured Despisers* (1799) is the classic attempt at contextualizing the Word of God for a secular humanist culture.

Traditionally, the problem of mediating Gospel to culture was the question of how to relate revelation and reason. How do we use the categories of human reason to interpret Divine revelation? A similar struggle occurs in the relationship between philosophy and theology. Some speak here about the work of translation as the "incarnation of the message." But we must be careful with this kind of language, for incarnation is about the Divine Word becoming human flesh, not merely human words. We don't speak of the Word becoming words. The stance we take concerning the relationship of Gospel to culture determines all our ensuing theological statements. Method determines content. This is especially true in the last hundred years as regards the doctrine of God's sovereignty. Two key concerns come to bear on this question: the first is the reality of God; the second is the kingship of God. On the one hand, the core of the biblical message is told in the first commandment: "There is no God beside me" (Is. 45:21). On the other hand, equally central to the biblical message is the advent of the kingdom of God: "Your God reigns" (Is. 52:7). These two aspects—God's unique reality and His kingship—are the essence of God's sovereignty, and together compose the central message of Scripture; they do not denote mere existence for God. All efforts at contextualizing the doctrine of God's sovereignty are conducted under high tension. For if in the translation of the message either of these aspects is impaired or lost—if one aspect is emphasized to the jeopardy or eclipse of the other—then the very Gospel itself is suppressed; God's sovereignty is denied, and, very often, man's sovereignty declared in its place.

Introduction

THE TENETS OF SECULARISM

The two philosophical bases of the Enlightenment, secularism and humanism, form a system that can be summarized in four points.

(1) The system's cornerstone is a critical self-limitation of reason that refuses to think about God, in order that man may seize power and declare autonomy. Scripture would call this "forgetting God."

(2) In this new autonomy, metaphysics, or transcendence, or "God," becomes redundant. Whatever is outside the sphere of this-worldliness is deemed superfluous. There are, of course, different responses to this assertion of human autonomy. One response is atheism, a complete rejection of the idea of God. Another is agnosticism, a refusal to embrace anything about God with firmness and finality. Yet another way to make the idea of God redundant is to reduce the tenets of theology to the tenets of anthropology, so that talk about God is interpreted as a kind of code language for talk about man.

(3) This new autonomy understands the universe in terms of a closed system of nature, explained by theories of evolution. These theories are materialistic: there is no need for God or spirit. But these theories are not always consistently materialistic: often there is in them a concealed teleology or doctrine of natural purposiveness, which sees man as nature's highest goal.

(4) Very often the new autonomy accepts what Martin Buber (1878–1965) has called the "I-Thou," but restricts it to a this-worldly inter-subjectivity.

So the Enlightenment system, the crucible in which modern theology is shaped, has these four tenets: human autonomy, the redundancy of transcendence, a resolute this-worldliness worked out in philosophical materialism and evolution, and a merely this-worldly inter-subjectivity.

This system pervades modern thought. In the theologies we will discuss, therefore, we will need to examine how those theologies interact with all or some of these tenets of the Enlightenment's secular humanism.

Meditation
Psalm 119:123-125

> My eyes fail, looking for your salvation,
>   looking for your righteous promise.
> Deal with your servant according to your love
>   and teach me your decrees.
> I am your servant; give me discernment
>   that I may understand your statutes.

Here the Psalmist is saying, "I have really tried to seek your salvation and understand your righteous word. I am at a point where my eyes seem to fail." Then he falls back to his claim, "I am your servant."

Some of you may be in a similar situation. You ask for a special insight, be it in terms of theology or your own future path. You come to a situation where you seem to have failed. You just can't perceive what the will of the Lord is. You can return to your original commitment (if it be in place), "I am your servant." That is your title to bang on the door. If he has accepted you as his servant, then you are entitled to get the specifics of that.

Chapter One

FRIEDRICH DANIEL ERNST SCHLEIERMACHER (1768–1834)

We will begin with the two main modes of modern Protestant systematic theology around the turn of the century: one is the liberal school and the other the evangelical alternative. We will start with Friedrich Schleiermacher, and then from him we will jump to the situation of theology at the end of the nineteenth century. But we must begin with Schleiermacher, for he is the prototype of all liberal theology. If you can understand Schleiermacher, you can design the next liberal theological system yourself. It is all there in him. Under one guise or another, in one dialect or another, liberal theologians are merely restating Schleiermacher.

SCHLEIERMACHER'S CONTEMPORARY INFLUENCE

As I have just suggested, to prepare the stage for a history of twentieth-century theology, it is necessary to go back to Friedrich Schleiermacher. He began the age of modern theology in 1799 with the publication of his book *On Religion: Speeches to its Cultured Despisers*. The theological battles that continue today can be traced back to him, and we might even say that all theological development since him has been either pro- or contra-Schleiermacher. He is the first great theologian of modernity, and has been called, with full right to the title, the church father of the nineteenth and twentieth centuries. He is the unsurpassed model—indeed, the archetype—of all modern liberal theology. He was the first to do theology under the conditions of the Enlightenment, and in an ingenious way showed how this could be done. He was the one who overcame the "defeat" inflicted upon traditional Protestant orthodoxy by Enlightenment rationalism. He represents a new departure. Theology was at a dead end before he wrote. It had died at the hands of rationalism.

Schleiermacher is also unsurpassed because he invented the idea of theological liberalism within the church. Prior to Schleiermacher, those within the church were expected to be orthodox. If you rejected orthodoxy, it was expected that you would leave the church. There were, to attenuate this tension, peace treaties between orthodox and liberal theology. One was a famous edict issued in 1796 by the Prussian minister of education, which allowed pastors to hold liberal views as a personal matter but required them to preach orthodoxy from the pulpit. But, in truth, liberalism was not congruent with churchmanship, and a better route for liberals was to leave the church entirely. Schleiermacher changed all that by bringing theological liberalism into the church.

"Liberalism" means freedom from dogmatic restriction on human reason. Schleiermacher pioneered the stance of being both a modern man and yet a convinced Christian at the same time; it is for this reason he has become the model for so many others. The way in which his theology was received also makes Schleiermacher a gateway into all subsequent Protestant theology. After his death, his

Friedrich Daniel Ernst Schleiermacher (1768–1834)

influence extended to all theological movements after him. He was influential even in the evangelical revival movement in the first third of the nineteenth century, a movement that was in some ways a continuation of Schleiermacher's philosophical sentiment that the emotions are the seat of religion. The subterranean link between Schleiermacher and the evangelical revival was the school of Romanticism, which we will explore in detail later. For now, we are simply tracing the streams of Schleiermacher's influence. But the irony of his influence on evangelicalism needs to be noted: supposedly fervent in their orthodoxy, evangelicals shared with Schleiermacher, the grandfather of liberalism, a deep conviction that religion is fundamentally a matter of the emotions. This conviction remains, down to our own day, the door through which Schleiermacher's theology enters into evangelical circles. Schleiermacher also powerfully influenced the mid-nineteenth century school of "Mediation Theology," so named because of the school's attempt to mediate between or harmonize church and culture. All these theologians were dependent on Schleiermacher. A third stream of Schleiermacher's influence comes through classic liberal theology, represented in the second half of the nineteenth century most prominently by Albrecht Ritschl (1822–1889). So, fifty years after Schleiermacher's death, there were three distinct streams of piety and theology flowing from his thought and theology: evangelicalism, mediation theology and liberal theology.

Only with Karl Barth (1886–1968) and the other "dialectical" theologians of the 1920s did a challenge to Schleiermacher's pervasive domination begin. The first salvo against Schleiermacher was *Mysticism and the Word* (1924) by Emil Brunner (1889–1966), who portrayed Schleiermacher's theology as a modern form of mysticism, and contrasted it with the Word of God; as Brunner put it, Christianity is about hearing, not feeling. Karl Barth was another exponent of the counter-reaction against Schleiermacher, both in his essays on Schleiermacher and in his *Protestant Theology in the Nineteenth Century* (1947). But the heyday of the dialectical theologians has passed; their influence has waned, and we again have been moved increasingly under the sway of Schleiermacher. The previous generation of theologians was dominated by people who, even if they did not name Schleiermacher, fundamentally repeated his theology. Paul Tillich (1886–1965), for example, is a direct theological heir of Schleiermacher, and the breadth of his influence in the twentieth century is similar to that of Schleiermacher's in the nineteenth. Rudolf Bultmann (1884–1976) and the school he spawned are also representatives of the Schleiermacherian system, sometimes repeating it almost verbatim. Gerhard Ebeling, the systematic theologian of the Bultmannian school, is very clearly in the tradition of Schleiermacher.

Even more recently there has been in North American liberal theology almost an explosion of the influence of Schleiermacher. This resurgent influence is evident in H. Richard Niebuhr, for example, who in 1964 heralded the rediscovery of Schleiermacher with his book *Schleiermacher on Christ and Religion*. The book is not a critical investigation, but rather an attempt to make Schleiermacher's theological approach fruitful once more in our own time. A second testimony to the resurgence of Schleiermacher's influence may be seen in the work of Peter L. Berger, today's most famous sociologist of religion; Berger makes Schleiermacher's "inductive" approach to religion normative for himself and for his own time. The noted ethicist James M. Gustafson provides a surprisingly clear resuscitation of Schleiermacher's doctrines of God and Christ. And even many young evangelicals often end up reinventing Schleiermacher as they emerge from their theological ghetto and encounter the "Christ and Culture"

Friedrich Daniel Ernst Schleiermacher (1768–1834)

problem for themselves—in the clash between the natural sciences and religion, for example, or the clash between the social sciences and religion. In their attempts to come up with a scheme of interaction they repeat, unaware that they are doing so, what Schleiermacher said two centuries ago.

Yet the most striking instances of Schleiermacher's resurgent influence and importance are the recent attempts by liberals and evangelicals to use his brand of subjectivist theology as the basis for a possible reconciliation. The idea is that these two warring camps can unite in the view, hailed by Schleiermacher, that religion is primarily a subjective experience. One such attempt at reunification occurred in a striking dialogue I heard at Harvard in 1981. Two liberal professors from Harvard, and two evangelical scholars (a church historian and a systematic theologian) ended up concluding that a reunification of liberal and evangelical Christianity was possible. The terms spelled out for reunification were exactly those of Schleiermacher's model for doing theology under the conditions of the Enlightenment—though Schleiermacher was never actually named as the founder of such theology. Such a reunification would have betrayed the Bible's objective Gospel because it would have embraced the brand of subjectivism that, though present in much evangelical theology, also animates modern liberalism. Liberalism is not always critical and rationalist; it also takes the form of subjectivism. Thus, Schleiermacher rules again. Ironically, even Catholic theologians are discovering him. When I was at Tübingen, for example, where a Protestant and a Roman Catholic school stand side by side, I heard Walter Kasper lecture on the subject, "Catholicism is the Best Protestantism that Ever Was." He basically reformulated the whole Roman Catholic synthesis of nature and grace in terms congruent with Schleiermacher and at the end of the lecture actually pointed to Schleiermacher as the model for future Catholic theology! I have heard from one of my former students, who is now at the University of Notre Dame, that Schleiermacher is "Number One" there. The very influential Catholic theologian Karl Rahner also gives Schleiermacher high praise. So Schleiermacher is very contemporary.

SCHLEIERMACHER'S LIFE

Schleiermacher's father was a Reformed army chaplain who began as a rationalist and liberal but became increasingly conservative in the course of his life. He wanted to safeguard his son's religious formation in a time of increasing rationalism, so he sent him to a Moravian Brethren school in Niesky. The strategy was so successful that at the end of his primary schooling at age 14, Schleiermacher decided after a night of prayer to join that communion. He then went to a Moravian seminary in Barby. Within a year, however, he was found with some friends secretly reading rationalist theological literature and had to leave the divinity program. In a famous letter to his father, he announces that he cannot believe in the divinity of Christ: it is not reasonable. He cannot believe Christ's substitutionary atonement: it is not reasonable. Sin is just weakness, a lack of good: it is not rebellion. If we were rebellious against God we would have to accuse God of having created us this way. Neither he nor his father really knew what to do at this point. At any rate, Schleiermacher continued to study theology, now (1787) at the university of Halle, and lived with his uncle, a moderately rationalist theology professor at the university.

In 1790, after Schleiermacher finished his theology degree, he became a tutor in a nobleman's family in western Prussia and again in that family encountered a very warm, personal faith. He was ordained to the clergy in 1794 and was appointed Reformed chaplain at Charité, the royal hospital in Berlin. Here he came right into the centre of

Friedrich Daniel Ernst Schleiermacher (1768–1834)

the literary movement of Romanticism, and into a centre of lively exchange of thoughts and sentiments. It was the time of the great literary hostesses, and in their salons Schleiermacher quickly gained a reputation as a brilliant young man. In 1799, he published his famous first book, *On Religion: Speeches to Its Cultured Despisers*, in which he applies the Romantic movement to religion; this book was not published in English until 1893. In the context of theology, Schleiermacher explored the most recent cultural ideas, and so became a pioneer in the Romantic movement. The work is a defense of religion against the attacks of rationalism but on the basis of Romanticism, a broad cultural movement stemming especially from Jean-Jacques Rousseau (1712–1778), characterized by the legitimacy of feeling, the right of freedom of form, and the creative imagination of the artistic or literary genius.

In the next year, Schleiermacher published *Soliloquies*, a series of monologues on philosophical ethics, rather less accessible than *On Religion*. *Letters About Lucinda* came next. This was a defense of a scandalous romanticist novel by Friedrich Schlegel (1772-1829), whom he knew at the Berlin literary salons. Schleiermacher said art must in no way be restricted by petty moral fences. Here we see the remarkable sight of one of the leading young theologians of the day defending what was at that time the most progressive form of literary pornography—an astonishing prefiguration of J. A. T. Robinson's defense in court of D. H. Lawrence's sexually frank *Lady Chatterly's Lover*, which became the best-known "sexually liberating" book of the 1960s.

Schleiermacher's next phase could be described as his coming of age emotionally. It was Romantically in-vogue to fall in love with educated, mature married women. Romantics didn't fall in love with teenagers, but with married women, especially the hostesses of the literary salons. In Schleiermacher's case, he fell in love with the wife of a fellow clergyman and even tried to persuade her to divorce her husband. (The divorce laws at that time were very lax.) Schleiermacher's bishop immediately sent him away to cool off in the cultural desert of Pomerania, a Prussian province on the Baltic Sea. In letters back to his mistress in Berlin, he continued to urge divorce but was unsuccessful. It was a sobering experience for Schleiermacher.

In 1804 he was made a professor at the university of Halle, where he worked very hard, producing several books on the philosophy of religion and ethics. After Napoleon's victory over the Prussian armies, the university was closed and he moved back to Berlin where he was celebrated for the patriotic sermons he preached. He married the young widow of one of his closest friends, and from then on led an exemplary family life. In 1809 he was made pastor at one of the major Berlin churches, and in 1810 became professor of theology at the new University of Berlin, the center of learning in Germany at that time. In 1810 he produced *Brief Outline of the Study of Theology*, and in 1821 his mature dogmatics, *The Christian Faith* (two volumes, revised in 1831). Posthumously, Schleiermacher's friends published his *Lectures on Christian Morals*, as well as other volumes. He was very influential and successful in church circles. He worked on the reform of liturgy and worship and on constitutional aspects of the church. And he was the driving force for the reunification of Lutherans and Reformed in the Union Church of Prussia in 1825. He was a leading figure inside the church, demonstrating the possibility of mingling thorough-going liberalism with fervent churchmanship.

EPISTEMOLOGICAL PRESUPPOSITIONS

Rationalism's Critique of Christianity

Schleiermacher was doing theology under siege. That is the background for understanding his attempt to renew theological inquiry: he was working beneath the weight of the Enlightenment's attack on Christianity. The Enlightenment and its rule of Reason had muted theology's voice. Schleiermacher rejected that. Instead, he launched a formidable reaction to Reason's dictatorship over religion, for rationalism had caused an enormous reduction of doctrine. This reductionism was the dominating principle of theology in the 18th century. Doctrine had been reduced by degrees, beginning with criticism of the concept of personal evil, Satan, which led to a rejection of the concept of hell. Then the doctrine of Christ's bodily resurrection came under scrutiny and contempt. The process of reduction began on the periphery and inched closer and closer to the center. The process continued until only Kant's three famous concepts of Enlightenment theology were left: God (with no detailed description), the concept of freedom (implying the demand for a morality of some kind), and the immortality of the soul (the residue of eschatology). The overall result was a reduction of religion to morality. At times one would speak about "religion" and mean by that the moral postulates of the Enlightenment. To be religious was to live a decent life. There were no metaphysical or transcendental elements, only morality.

The Critique of Philosophical Theology by Kant

The critique by the Enlightenment was perfected in the critical philosophy of Immanuel Kant (1724–1804). His three mature works of later life completed the Enlightenment critique. These were his *Critique of Pure Reason* (1781), *Critique of Practical Reason* (1788), and *Critique of Judgment* (1790). *The Critique of Pure Reason* is the most important for our purposes. Like Goethe and Barth, Kant had two professional lives: long before he published these works he was a very famous man. Some people, like Kant, are successful more than once. Kant, after publishing his great philosophical trilogy, applied his insights directly to religion in the famous small monograph *Religion Within the Limits of Reason Alone* (1793). This little booklet gives an accurate feel for what lies behind much modern theology.

What does Kant do in these books? Prior to Kant, the Enlightenment had reduced religion from supernature to nature, from revelation to reason. Kant takes this reduction as an established thing, and thus proceeds to test the boundaries of reason as they pertain to religion. He tries to determine what a rational religion can contain: what, in terms of faith, can be proved? Kant, in this exploration, leaves revelation by the side. He is only interested in what a "rational faith" looks like, or what in religion we can affirm on the basis of the Enlightenment.

In the *Critique of Pure Reason*, Kant wreaks critical destruction on rational religion, on philosophical theology, on natural theology—that is, on any religion or theology articulated by reason alone, without recourse to revelation or tradition. At the heart of this critical destruction of philosophical theology is Kant's attack on the traditional rational proofs for God's existence: the ontological, the cosmological, and the teleological proofs. According to Kant, all philosophical arguments for the existence of God are merely extrapolations of this-worldly phenomena. The concepts of God which these so-called proofs establish are only personifications of thought concepts. Kant says the idea of God is desirable, indeed indispensable for philosophy (because it is one of the ideas that rationality requires or implies), but God's existence cannot be proved. Proof, for Kant, means scientific proof—that is, rational considerations of sense experience. Here is the beginning of modernity.

Kant's destruction of the traditional arguments for the existence of God had a dramatic consequence: it forced a strict division between this world and the other world, an

Friedrich Daniel Ernst Schleiermacher (1768–1834)

iron curtain between phenomena (things experienced by sense perception) and noumena (things that are thought). We cannot know what is beyond the reach of our sense experience. The result—the intentional result—of Kant's critique is a kind of agnosticism. God's existence can neither be rationally proved nor rationally disproved. Kant believed that this argument does religion a great service because it shows that atheism is rationally impossible. No rational proofs—empirically verifiable facts, logically valid arguments—can be presented either for God's existence or against God's existence. God's existence or non-existence must be taken on sheer faith.

The Moral Postulate of God

The result of Kant's first critique is the refutation of rational theology. His next book, *Critique of Practical Reason*, takes up the question of morality and thus moral theology. Having refuted in his first critique any attempt at basing theology in metaphysical reasoning about sensory experience, Kant suddenly comes back in his second critique with a "postulate"—a necessary presupposition, not a rational proof—for the existence of God. His argument runs as follows. Though we cannot prove God's existence in metaphysics, in the field of morality we are nevertheless forced to postulate or assume that God exists. This is not a metaphysical but a moral argument. Why is it necessary to assume the existence of God in ethics? There are two reasons. The first is that man is evil. If he is to act with inner moral rightness, and not merely in accord with external legal rightness, man first needs to undergo regeneration, "a revolution of his whole way of thinking." This regeneration can only come from something like God. Apart from the existence of God, one vainly hopes that people will ever act in a truly moral way.

Behind Kant's statement here, there is a historical factor which gives weight to his argument. Kant was speaking about man's need for "a revolution of his whole way of thinking" during the time of the French Revolution. He is saying, in other words, that it is foolish to hope for any betterment of society by means of political revolution, by a mere change of social structures. Man is evil. Kant saw that political revolutions do not achieve morality: only an inner revolution can do that. Here he affirms the doctrine of original sin; in fact, he makes that doctrine the starting point for his ethics. Many of Kant's critics wonder how he, being an Enlightened person, could make such an assumption. Presumably, they suppose, it is a holdover from his pietistic upbringing. We will return to this question.

There is, according to Kant, a second reason why we need to postulate the existence of God. In order for morality to make sense, there must be hope that the good will be vindicated one day. Otherwise the course of things in the empirical world makes moral life unrewarding. We need the hope that after this life the ideal will be implemented in reality. Kant said, "I need God as the guarantor of the victory of the good."

By continuing to deny the validity of rational proofs for God's existence as regards the empirical phenomena of the sensory world, Kant's religion of ethical monotheism based in his moral arguments for God's existence constitute a religion "within the limits of reason alone"—a religion congruent with the principles of the Enlightenment. Kant thus tried to replace with moral theology the rational theology that he considered to have been refuted by the Enlightenment, especially by David Hume (1711–1776), who awoke Kant from his "dogmatic slumber."

Friedrich Daniel Ernst Schleiermacher (1768–1834)

The Agnostic Response to Kant

What was the response of the public to Kant's critiques? The public accepted his critique of rational theology but rejected his moral postulate of God. They rallied about him in his work of demolition, but abandoned him in his attempt at restoration. Why? There were two reasons. First, they rejected the philosophical presupposition of man's inherent sinfulness. They disagreed with his resuscitation of the doctrine of original sin. In the 18th century, people were more likely to exclaim over their own goodness than to lament over their sin. The great spokesman of the time was the German poet Goethe (1749–1832), who asserted, "By assuming man's sinfulness, Kant has stained his philosopher's mantle." The second reason for rejecting Kant's moral postulate was furnished, unwittingly, by Kant himself. What his critics did was to take his own critique of philosophical religion and turn it against the idea of the moral postulate. Is not, they asked, the moral postulate just another personification of a thought concept? Is it not another projection of human need? The overall result of Kant's intervention on the side of religion is that God is banned from philosophy and ethics, in both thought and action. This sad state of affairs is the starting point for Schleiermacher's vindication of religion.

Schleiermacher published his first book, *On Religion: Speeches to its Cultured Despisers*, in 1799, when he was 31, four years before Kant's death. The young Schleiermacher accepted the state of affairs brought on by Kant. Theory and practice, science and morality had all become completely secular. If there is no longer room for religion in philosophy and science on the one hand, and in ethics, politics and morality on the other, does this mean we must become atheists? Schleiermacher's answers that question in his first book. Here, he joins with the general public development of thought, but he also pioneers new roads. He breaks new ground in Romanticism's revolt against the 18th century's reign of rationalism. He is not simply a fellow-traveler of this new movement, but one of its prophets: his book is one of the manifestos of Romanticism's victory over rationalism. The book has five chapters. The first part is an apology or defense. The second discusses the nature of religion. The third is on religious education. The fourth deals with association in religion (church, priesthood). The fifth treats the plurality of religions.

Underpinning these chapters is the question: Must we become atheists? What is the answer? The answer is no. Rather than become atheists, we must redeploy religion into the area of feeling and sentiment. For Schleiermacher, religion has nothing to do with science or ethics or politics. Religion does not really belong at all in the fields of morals or metaphysics. It is neither the master nor the servant of science or politics. However, religion has its own "peculiar territory" in the "higher feelings"; this is religion's "province of its own in the mind." Schleiermacher accepts the Enlightenment's elimination of religion from science and philosophy, politics and ethics—the provinces of reason and will. Rather than trying to recapture lost territory, he redeploys religion into feeling, another "province." If you lack this province, Schleiermacher claims, you are not a fully developed human being. So all who are genuinely "cultured," "all better souls," respect religion, and indeed appropriate and cultivate it. "But while man does nothing from religion, he should do everything with religion. Uninterruptedly, like sacred music, the religious feelings should accompany his active life." An existence without the "music" of religion is impoverished, atrophied. So whoever is truly educated and cultured must be deeply religious.

Did Schleiermacher really make an advance? In some ways we can say he did. His strategy was a retreat that was also an advance, like the long march of the Chinese

Friedrich Daniel Ernst Schleiermacher (1768–1834)

communists to Sinkiang under the pressure of the Japanese and the nationalist Chinese armies. He withdrew from the provinces that he felt could no longer be held. He claims that those other two provinces, reason and will, never rightly belonged to religion anyway. This looks in every way like a full retreat, but at the time it was an advance insofar as it put religion back into currency. Schleiermacher's approach was in this regard utterly successful: religion became popular.

Schleiermacher proposed a definition of religion: "The immediate feeling of the Infinite and Eternal"; "True religion is sense and taste for the Infinite." Religion here is reduced to perception and emotion. We need to look at this definition's emphasis on subjective experience, but also at Schleiermacher's choice of language to describe the object of that experience. With regard to the emphasis on subjectivity, Schleiermacher defines religion as "having a taste for," having an "intuition," an "experience." The nature of that experience is, according to him, having a sudden sense of the hugeness and wholeness of being, a glimpse of the universe's completeness and interconnectedness. That is religion. To indicate what he means by religion, Schleiermacher points to experiences in which the "magical contact" of a single particular object transforms one's awareness of that object into an awareness of the Universe as a whole. This might, for example, be the experience, both commonplace and yet exhilarating, of seeing one early morning the whole beauty of the Universe distilled in the brilliance of a single dew drop. As the English poet William Blake (1757–1827) put the Romantic vision: "To see the world in a grain of sand / And a heaven in a wild flower, / Hold infinity in the palm of your hand / And eternity in an hour." The experience is wider and deeper than mere "nature," for it involves one's own unity with the Universe. Religion, then, is the emotional encounter with the whole of Being: "Your whole life is such an existence for self in the Whole." Both the self and the object merge and become one in such "holy wedlock": "You lie directly on the bosom of the infinite world. In that moment you are its soul . . . [and] it is your body." Schleiermacher admits that such experiences are volatile, mere fleeting moments. But that is his key description of religion: a sudden experience of the depth of being, of being at one with the Universe.

Sense, sentiment, feeling, emotion, piety, experience—these are Schleiermacher's subjectivistic terms. The Whole, the Infinite, the Universe—these are his key terms to describe the object of belief and experience. It is important to note that in the German language these terms are all capitalized and nominalized adjectives; they are all in the neutral gender. Never once does Schleiermacher use the term "God" in *On Religion*, but only "the godhead." He thus removes all personal content from the object of belief, and reduces God to a vague, amorphous something. The object of religious experience is not an entity, a person, but a quality. Here Schleiermacher comes very close to pantheism.

Schleiermacher's Re-Interpretation of Christianity

We can summarize *On Religion* by looking at the fifth speech, which concerns religious pluralism. Here Schleiermacher speaks of Christianity's place among other religions. Let us recall that he sets out to vindicate not Christianity but religion—religion as a sentiment for and a sense of the Infinite. And if that is religion, then, of course, it must have many individual forms. One task of theology must become seeking the genuine intuition of the Infinite in each of the various individual forms. Since there must be many religions, only the sum of them encompasses the Truth: "The whole of religion is nothing but the sum of all relations of man to God, apprehended in all the possible ways in which any man can be immediately conscious in

Friedrich Daniel Ernst Schleiermacher (1768–1834)

this life." The genius of Christianity is that it is the most perfect, the most remarkable, of all religions.

Christianity is highest among all religions because it describes the eternal action of the divine in terms of salvation. The Christian doctrine of salvation is important because it makes human weakness, the human inability to be religious, its particular topic, and offers a cure for that. Christ was the first to comprehend the general corruption of religion in humanity, and Christ promises salvation from that corruption. The recognition of humankind's essential religious weakness becomes Christianity's central insight, and Schleiermacher says that this insight would last even if Christianity itself were to disappear. He claims Christianity does not even wish to rule alone, but appreciates diversity both within and outside itself. A truly religious person will welcome new things, expecting younger, stronger, and perhaps more beautiful forms of religion to arise. Nothing, according to him, is more irreligious, more un-Christian, than to demand uniformity in religion.

How does Schleiermacher's revolution change the meaning of divine revelation? Schleiermacher, we have seen, claims that religion takes place at the juncture where the Infinite reveals itself to us and we comprehend that "revelation." Such a revelation of the Infinite occurs, for instance, when we encounter the Universe in some act or entity of nature. A second level where we experience that revelation is in humanity, especially in the history of humanity: the Infinite can disclose itself in all the jostle and tumult of history, in all its wondrous richness and variety of people and event. Third, and especially, we can expect the Infinite to reveal itself in ourselves, in our own inner world. When some seemingly normal experience of life suddenly speaks to us with a deeper meaning, when an individual phenomenon enlarges, transforms, to become an image of the whole Universe—that is the moment of revelation. So "revelation" does not take place exclusively, or even usually, in religious contexts, such as the reading of Scripture, or the discipline of prayer or fasting. Rather, it is capricious and wide-ranging, breaking in upon any of us in our contemplation of nature and history, or in the confines of our own psyche. Heaven mingles suddenly with earth, the sublime invades the mundane. Yet revelation is not something God—or the Infinite—does independently of us: revelation depends not on what God speaks or shows, but on what we feel or perceive. It is exclusively human-centred. Apart from man, God can do nothing. Clearly, then, according to this loose and subjective definition, there are many revelations. Revelation is ongoing and available to all. Schleiermacher dismisses the orthodox belief that a revelation to some particular person or persons can be authoritative—even it if enshrined in a holy book. Each person must have his or her own experience of the Universe. Better to experience personally, immediately, the fiery molten rock of the Infinite than to study the cold hard lava of some extinct volcano. The most truly religious person, in fact, is the one who can most easily do without the dead reports of someone else's religious experience. Hence, revelation not only can, but must take place today. To be truly religious, you yourself must experience the Infinite.

What does Schleiermacher's revolution do to eschatology? Here Schleiermacher heralds the modern liberal eschatological position: the soul's "immortality" becomes a quality of life in the present, not a continuation of life after death. Such eschatology of the present will later come to prominence in theologians like Rudolf Bultmann. As Schleiermacher says at the end of the second speech, "In the midst of finitude to be one with the Infinite, and in every moment to be eternal is the immortality of religion." It is the religious depth of our present life, not the promise of an

Friedrich Daniel Ernst Schleiermacher (1768–1834)

afterlife, which is immortality. It is a qualitative concept of time, not a concept of time relating to eternity.

How does Schleiermacher change the meaning of "miracle"? There is in Schleiermacher no emphasis on the historical element in religion, the roots of Christianity. Schleiermacher has no use for the New Testament Greek word *ephapax*, "once for all"—that is, the historical moment of salvation. But he does not reject the concept of miracle—instead, he enlarges, and flattens, the concept to include everything: "To me all is a miracle," since everything finite "is a sign of the Infinite," and therefore the term "miracle" is "simply the religious name for event." As with divine revelation, "miracle" thus becomes redefined not in terms of God's actions but in terms of human perception and interpretation: "miracle" or "wonder" (German: *Wunder*) "refers purely to the mental condition of the observer…. The more religious you are, the more miracle would you see everywhere." Later, Schleiermacher will suggest that everything is miraculous with a view to divine providence: God is the one who provides for the life of the Universe, and since everything depends upon God, everything must be miraculous.

Finally, what does Schleiermacher's revolution mean for our understanding of God himself? The subjective side in religion becomes decisive. The objective reality of God does not matter much any more. For Schleiermacher, a belief in a personal God is not better than belief in an impersonal God. A Being outside the world, a Being with consciousness and will—all that is secondary. What matters is the subject's strength of feeling. Belief in a personal God is not harmful, but it is not necessary. Nowhere does Schleiermacher use the term "God" positively. The closest he gets is "deity," with overtones of unknowability. God fades into the background. Schleiermacher summarized all this in a famous quote: "It matters not what conceptions [of God] a man adheres to, he can still be pious," and that is what matters. The first edition of *On Religion* is far more radical than later editions, on which the English translation is based and which accommodated reactions from his ecclesiastical superiors and the church. But in the first edition he says, "Faith in God depends only on the direction of one's fantasy." If your fantasy is conditioned to personify everything, fine. But don't find fault with those who don't need such personification since they can think in terms of the spirit of the Universe.

The proposition of religion as subjectivity creates a redundant, unnecessary, superfluous God, a God who is merely an attribute of things and events which happen anyway. "Every event, even the most natural and usual, becomes a miracle, as soon as the religious view of it can be dominant." Religion occurs at the juncture not where God breaks in upon the world but where we subjectively perceive the world in a certain way. The Infinite, the Universe, affects us and creates emotions in us: the emotions are what matter. Later, therefore, Schleiermacher will speak of God as the co-determinant: God does not reach into history, but rather is co-determinant with natural developments; God is simply a different interpretation of natural developments, a matter of interpretation. The second Speech gives one indication why Schleiermacher undertakes this line of argument: It is "the metaphysicians and moralists in religion" that have brought "religion into discredit" by arguing in ways that "trespassed on the universal validity of scientific and physical conclusions." Genuine religion, for Schleiermacher, never trespasses on the territory of the sciences because it is only an interpretation subjectively added to events: "Religion leaves your physics untouched, and please God, also your psychology." This is a very far-reaching observation. It is almost a prophecy of the dialectical theology that would emerge a hundred years later. Working within such theology, Barth and Bultmann said it is no good to withdraw religion from the field of science into our interior, because the psychologists of religion will follow you there and explain your religious experiences scientifically too, as they do any other phenomena. Bultmann narrowed religious experience almost to the point of a needle, so that not even psychological categories can get hold of it; this way religion is to be safe from scientific critique. We will examine this later. At this point we need note only that Schleiermacher anticipates these developments and wants to find a refuge for religion that not even Sigmund Freud eighty years later will be able to get into and destroy.

Schleiermacher's Transformation

As rationalism attacked and destroyed the objects of religious belief, Schleiermacher withdrew religion into the sphere of subjectivity to shield it from the rationalist critique. Characteristically, he tells religion's cultured despisers, "Permit me to speak of myself." Of all our varied languages, theology should speak of God, but Schleiermacher sees theology as a way of speaking about the self. In another famous sentence from the first Speech, we read that piety "helped me as I began to sift the faith of my fathers and to cleanse thought and feeling from the rubbish of antiquity. When the God and the immortality of my childhood vanished from my doubting eyes, [piety] remained to me." Religion, then, is a matter of personal experience. It does not involve holding to certain propositions. Religion, rather, is devotion. We are not to ask, "Devoted to what?" Just be devout. Religion is not caught up in objective doctrines, but concerns the strength and intensity and warmth of human feeling. It is easy to see how this emphasis recommends itself to the unsuspecting evangelical, because evangelicals have always had an interest in experience and warmth of feeling. In the ensuing generations, it was evangelicals who transmitted this emphasis in Schleiermacher's theology.

Nevertheless, we must admit that Schleiermacher's transformation of the meaning of "religion" was immediately successful in re-establishing religion as a legitimate subject of public interest. Religion became part of educated social life again. Everybody—the churches, evangelicalism—profited by this renewed interest in religion.

Yet perhaps it was not a regenerated Christianity which overcame the Enlightenment. Maybe Schleiermacher offered only a religious version of Romanticism, which should have been expected anyway, once rationalism had run its course, having devoured all religious objects and leaving human beings naked and needy. Moreover, religion's victory through Schleiermacher's re-interpretation was empty: the movement of science toward independence from God was not reversed. The science of the nineteenth century was still very much an atheistic enterprise. And neither did Schleiermacher arrest the movement of politics done apart from God, though this was his intention. His idea was that if we remove religion from contested fields then we sidestep quarrels we cannot win and so prevent the spread of atheism. What actually happened, though, was that he removed Christianity as an ethical factor just at the point when it was most needed—at the point of early capitalism and rapid industrialization. When he said religion has nothing to do with ethics, Schleiermacher deprived Christianity from any social and political impact. Christianity in Continental Europe could have been, as it earlier had been in England during the Wesleyan revival, a corrective to the situation of rapid industrialism. Admittedly, Schleiermacher didn't adhere to this position. In later years, he came to recognize Christians' social responsibility: he taught ethics and did pioneering work for social legislation. But this focus came too late to undo the pervasive cultural influence of his famous book *On Religion*, which was of course intended for the cultured or educated classes of Christian (or formerly Christian) Europe.

SCHLEIERMACHER'S MATURE SYSTEM

The Heritage of the Reformation

We have discussed Schleiermacher's early landmark work *On Religion: Speeches to Its Cultured Despisers* (1799), where he first tries to re-establish religion as a major public concern in the era of the Enlightenment and the response of Romanticism. The next work in the reconciliation of Christianity to his time comes several years later with the publication of *The Christian Faith According to the Principles of the Protestant Church* in 1821. This book is a comprehensive dogmatics based in Schleiermacher's subjectivistic theology. It is complex and dense, but, to give it its due, it is very beautifully conceived. In this work Schleiermacher takes theology to be an empirical, even a statistical, discipline, since he assigns it the task of accounting for the beliefs of the church at a point of time—namely, his own. This method has far-reaching importance. By confining himself simply to describing Christianity in the present age, he neatly disposes of the whole question of absolute truth and authority in theology—the very things that otherwise would cause him trouble in his modernist and subjectivist presentation. By seeking only to describe the Christian faith commonly held in his own day, Schleiermacher clearly holds to the concept of what he calls "living Christianity," a concept that allows for an evolution in belief or faith. He bases his dogmatics not primarily on Scripture, but on documents of the Reformation. For Schleiermacher, these documents possess in a number of places a clarity that is lacking in the New Testament. They are a step beyond the New Testament in that they better explain our faith. He claims he will return to the New Testament only when the confessional documents are insufficiently specific. In this approach, tradition supersedes Scripture; Schleiermacher himself was astonished that his reviewers didn't accuse him of using Catholic methodology.

And Schleiermacher pushes the methodology yet further! For him, the concept of a progressive or evolutionary faith means that we must also frequently go beyond the writings of the Protestant Reformation. Hence, we must go beyond the Reformational documents into the "contemporary Protestant consciousness." Like Scripture, the confessional documents of the Reformation cannot be the final standard for determining the shape and content of Christian faith. The theologian alone ultimately decides the nature of the contemporary God-consciousness that the faithful hold in common. Thus, though statistics determine the present content of Christian faith, it is the theologian who decides what factors are actually to be determinative. Even a casual reading of *The Christian Faith* shows that for Schleiermacher the Reformation does not bind him. For example, he rejects the doctrine of the Trinity. In fact, he is quite anti-trinitarian and comes close to Unitarianism. His objection is that the Trinity never becomes an object of pious consciousness. No one ever experiences the Trinity. This is an implicitly Kantian statement, only in Romantic garb, since Kant also rejected the Trinity because he could not reduce the concept to something practical in our lives. (It is interesting to witness the different, in fact quite opposite, conclusions that theologians draw from the doctrine of the Trinity today. In 1980, Jürgen Moltmann published *The Trinity and the Kingdom of God*, and suddenly the Trinity became a highly important theological concept not only in dogmatics but also in theological ethics, where the Trinity became the guarantor of human social nature. The Trinity was the archetype of human togetherness: human community was seen as an analogy of the higher heavenly reality; and, as a result, it became utterly obligatory to base Christian social ethics on the idea of the Trinity. In the course of a hundred years since Schleiermacher, then, thinking on this doctrine has been completely reversed.)

Schleiermacher also opposes the Reformation's affirmation of Athanasius (296–373), who defended the divinity of Christ against Arianism, according to which the Logos or Word is an instrument made by God for the creation of the world. Schleiermacher is, in other words, exercising the now popular liberal option of rejecting Christ's divinity. Wherever we look in liberal theology, we encounter doubt—if not outright rejection—of any claim that Jesus Christ was divine. This topic, which is debated every ten years, was also part of Schleiermacher's pioneering work. Furthermore, Schleiermacher breaks with the Reformation in embracing universalism (the doctrine that in the end all will be saved). Martin Luther in his famous Confession of 1528 said, "I do not side with those who teach that even the devils will finally come to salvation." That statement defines universalism a bit sharply, but captures well the Reformation position, which Schleiermacher strongly rejects. In addition, he also directly contradicts the teaching of the whole church when he declares that God is the author of sin and evil. Schleiermacher holds this view because he wants to explain everything that happens in terms of God's causality and God's provision. He argues that this is a necessary stance if we are to believe God is omnipotent. But the express position of the Reformation documents was that God is not the creator or author of sin and evil. Schleiermacher's most glaring opposition to the Reformation, however, is his outright rejection of the Law. The Reformation taught both Law and Gospel. Yet Schleiermacher holds that the Law, especially as expressed in the Ten Commandments, is useless for the Christian because it is unsuitable as a description of the Christian life of sanctification.

In the light of these examples of Schleiermacher's rejection of basic Protestant doctrines, we must say that his methodological claim to hold to the Reformation documents is seriously in doubt.

The Basis for Theology in The Christian Faith

For Schleiermacher, the doctrines of the Christian faith are not developed from a survey of nature; they do not derive from the Jesus of history (Schleiermacher is not concerned with history at all) or from Scripture. Instead, contemporary Christian consciousness is the basis of faith. Schleiermacher thinks in terms of the timeless, living Christ dwelling in various ways in believers and in the church. Indeed, in a letter to an ecclesiastical superior he said, "I believe I know where our deepest dissension is. You believe in a revelation of God in Scripture. I couldn't be further from that position. I believe in a revelation of God in Christ." This way, of course, he is free to define "Christ" according to his own contemporary insights. Scripture is for him a secondary thing at best.

What is taking place here? Here we have the heart of the modern system of liberalism: the decision to begin with experience and only then move to Scripture. Experience always remains authoritative in the study of Scripture. Surprisingly, this approach has roots in Calvinism, since Calvin's doctrine of Scripture has two parts. Whenever someone becomes a Christian it is by the agreement of two witnesses: first there is Scripture and preaching, and secondly the inner testimony of the Holy Spirit. Calvin is clear that he does not think there is a separate voice speaking within us; it is, rather, a case of the Word, whether written or preached, entering the heart and finding an echo there. So we do not actually have two different witnesses

Friedrich Daniel Ernst Schleiermacher (1768–1834)

coming from different directions: there are two witnesses coming in tandem, one after the other; the Spirit follows the Word and confirms it. Now, this understanding can be misinterpreted through an over-emphasis on the preached Word in a manner that stifles the inner testimony of the Holy Spirit. But this understanding can also be misinterpreted in the other direction, toward dispensing with the guiding function of Scripture altogether, and it is in this direction that Schleiermacher moves. He emphasizes, to the detriment of the authority of Scripture, the inner testimony of the Holy Spirit, that is, on what the subject feels and thinks. It is interesting that Schleiermacher was by background a Calvinist and not a Lutheran; he held a Calvinist pulpit in Berlin. The doctrine of the inner testimony, so prominent in Calvinism, proved useful as he gave theology a subjectivistic foundation.

Today some evangelical theologians have become heirs to Schleiermacher in this matter, for there are now evangelicals who turn to Scripture only secondarily. Their method is first to experience the things of God, and then later to see whether one's experience can be supported somewhere in Scripture. If it isn't, so much the worse for Scripture. Schleiermacher, we must remember, shapes his understanding of faith from our common experience in the church. He begins with existing piety, the religious feelings that in fact are occurring in the communion of a church. According to Schleiermacher, to be pious one must become "an object to oneself" for one's own subjective consideration, in accordance with the intellectual "level of reflection" of which one is capable. One must study what one's feelings and experiences are. One's primary object of study is oneself, not Scripture.

As regards theological method, Schleiermacher says there are three forms of expression for doctrine. The first form is to express all the topics of dogmatics in terms of the conditions of human religion or piety. Here we have theology as the account of religious experience. This is Schleiermacher's own way of doing theology and therefore is, by his standards, theology's basic form. The second form is to describe the doctrine of God (the Divine attributes, the Divine actions) using metaphysical language. This is theology as salvation history. The third form is to make statements about the constitution of the world or cosmos as such, which is theology as cosmology. According to Schleiermacher, the first form is fundamental. We must do theology in terms of the phenomena of religion or piety, as a "presentation of ecclesiastical opinions." For him, theologies based on God's action or that look to the structure of the cosmos—the second and third forms specified—are dispensable. He anticipates a time when the churches will uphold a theology free of any reference to God's salvific acts in history and free of any reference to cosmology; but because of the conditions that obtained in the churches of his time, where people had not become accustomed to experiential theology, Schleiermacher articulates a theology that still entertains those modes of theological expression. Nevertheless, Schleiermacher's theology can be fully expressed in terms of religious anthropology without reference to cosmological transcendence or the history of salvation.

This basic subjectivism comes out even in the title of Schleiermacher's systematic theology. There is a hidden meaning in his change from the traditional title "Christian dogmatics" or "Christian doctrine" to "Christian faith." The word *Glaube* (belief, faith) is ambiguous here. It can be understood either in objective terms (a body of doctrine for belief) or in subjective terms (the kind of belief that I have). Under cover of this ambiguity, Schleiermacher is moving from an objectively based belief to a subjective understanding, which focuses not on the object of faith but

Friedrich Daniel Ernst Schleiermacher (1768–1834)

on the faith that I have within me. Since Schleiermacher, it has been said that Christian theology can no longer claim to state a knowledge of God or a doctrine of God, but only a knowledge of faith in God or a doctrine of Christian belief in God. In *The Christian Faith* as in *On Religion* Schleiermacher comes very close to saying that Christian doctrine is a product of the human spirit and not the revelation of God.

Schleiermacher's Reasons for the Re-founding of Theology

We turn to Schleiermacher's remarkably open "Letters to Dr Lücke," which were published in 1829. Prior to the publication of the second edition of *The Christian Faith* (1830), Schleiermacher in these letters gives an account of how he dealt with the critique provoked by the first edition. He describes the deepest principles and decisions behind the edition of 1832. The first part is in answer to his critics, and shows the impression the book made on contemporary readers. Schleiermacher claims that he is only describing the contemporary religious consciousness, his main concern. Indeed, according to Schleiermacher's own principles, he should place a high value on readers' responses: if contemporary piety is determinative for faith, as it was for Schleiermacher, then he should listen intently to what other Christians say.

The first criticism leveled is that Schleiermacher promoted pantheism. (Anyone who had read the book would arrive at this conclusion.) His reply is that this critique is based on *On Religion*, his first book; he simply observes this that book has been very well-received, and he has no regrets for writing it.

Secondly, critics attacked his concept of God, saying that his understanding of God was somewhat neo-Platonic. In his letters, Schleiermacher distinguishes between a God who is above all change, the cause of everything, but very much hidden, and a God who is subject to time. The latter is the theology of Pseudo-Dionysius the Areopagite, a monophysite Christian neo-Platonist in the sixth century whose books were attributed to the Dionysius mentioned in Acts 17:34. In this teaching, there is one God, the Platonic God, who is unknowable, and a half-man, half-God who is subject to time. Stated simply, Schleiermacher carries the duality between time and eternity into his concept of God. In response to this criticism, Schleiermacher simply denies being a neo-Platonist.

The third complaint was that Schleiermacher was also doing away with the historicity of Christ and was thereby changing theology into a kind of gnosis or mystical knowledge that has no relationship to historical reality. Here Schleiermacher faced no less a critic than the leading New Testament scholar of that generation, F. C. Baur (1792–1860). In his early years, Baur had been a disciple of Schleiermacher and was himself far more radically rationalist than his teacher. Yet it is Baur that maintains the authentically Christian point of view, based on the New Testament, that the historicity of Christ is central: "If everything is made dependent upon the life of Christ in us, then the death of Christ, and with it the whole historical person of Christ, must appear superfluous." When Schleiermacher tells Lücke that this criticism is based on a complete misunderstanding of his position, Schleiermacher invents a format that many of his twentieth-century followers have repeated when they have been criticized. (For example, when a critic seemed dangerously penetrating on a particular question during the demythologization debates of the 1950s, Rudolf Bultmann dodged the question at issue and simply said, "That fellow hasn't understood a single thing," and thus implied that the critic had no theological competence at all.) But if someone as brilliant as Baur didn't understand Schleiermacher, who will? Can this theologian even express himself intelligibly?

Friedrich Daniel Ernst Schleiermacher (1768–1834)

Thus, Schleiermacher did not answer but only deflected the three main criticisms of his theology.

The letters to Lücke also show the method underlying *The Christian Faith*. Schleiermacher foresees a clash between religion and science or research: "Shall the knot of history be thus loosed: Christianity with barbarism and learning with unbelief?" Rejecting such a conclusion, he sees it as theology's task to avert this clash by arranging an "eternal covenant" between Christianity and modern learning:

> If the Reformation, from whose first beginnings our Church took its life, has not the aim of establishing an eternal covenant between the living faith and scientific research, which is free to explore upon all sides and works for itself independently, so that faith does not hinder research, and research does not preclude faith: if it has not this aim then it is not adequate for the needs of our age and we require another Reformation, no matter how, and as a result of what struggles may develop. I am, however, firmly convinced that the basis for this covenant was already laid in those days, and that all that is needed is to bring about a more definite awareness on our part of that task in order to be able to achieve it.

If we wish to do more than to barricade ourselves against scientific research behind walls like the Roman Catholic authorities, we must discard all non-essentials in dogmatics and reformulate what remains. He tells Lücke, therefore, that his aim in the first edition of *The Christian Faith*, was to prove "that every dogma truly representing an element of our Christian awareness can also be formulated in such a way that it leaves us uninvolved with science." That is, the whole of dogmatics must be scrutinized toward distilling an essence of Christianity that cannot conflict with science. This famous phrase, the "essence of

Christianity"—which became the title of books by Ludwig Feuerbach (1841) and Adolf Harnack (1900)—is a guiding concept also for Schleiermacher. It describes his theological project: determining the essence or core of Christianity, and eliminating everything else. For Schleiermacher it is even necessary to do away with non-essentials in Scripture: the entire Old Testament (because it is an outmoded covenant for a particular nation), the creation in six days, and even the notion of creation itself (because the idea of Divine creation out of nothing cannot be rationally maintained). He wanted to re-organize the materials of Christian theology around Divine providence (understood as the sustaining of the universe) rather than around creation, since Divine providence can be considered a timeless, eternally occurring thing, whereas creation out of nothing cannot be.

The distillation of Christianity's "essence" also involves re-interpreting the New Testament miracles since, in his view, historical research can be sure of so few of them. Even if the miracles did happen it would be to our best advantage to re-interpret them in terms of natural analogies. We must get away from claiming their uniqueness, and we must reject the idea that God intrudes into history and breaks his own laws of nature. And the miracle of miracles, the death and resurrection of Christ, must also be re-understood—not as God entering into history and doing something completely new, but as a higher evolution of the spirit of humanity. Jesus Christ is not God incarnate.

Schleiermacher says, as well, that we must question the authenticity of some of the New Testament epistles. Indeed, if we are to change theology in the way that he deems necessary, we cannot uphold a canon of Holy Writings as authoritative and binding. Yet at the end, of course, he somehow maintains Christ and our faith in Christ remain the same.

Friedrich Daniel Ernst Schleiermacher (1768–1834)

Examples of Schleiermacher's Theological Reduction

(a) *God as ultimate cause.* We observe Schleiermacher's insistence that human experience has to be the starting point for theology in his famous development of the concept of God, which is found at the beginning of *The Christian Faith*. There he says that the "common element" in all the "diverse expression of piety" is "the consciousness of being absolutely dependent, or, which is the same thing, of being in relation with God." For Schleiermacher, therefore, the word "God" designates the "Whence" (the wherefrom, cause, origin, source) of our existence, upon which we feel to be essentially dependent rather than from which we feel to be essentially free. Everybody, he claims, feels dependencies in life. The newborn baby is of course almost totally dependent on his or her parents. But it is not an absolute dependence because there is also a little dependence the other way round: if an infant cries desperately, the parent tends to the child; the parent becomes dependent on what the child does. So there is no absolute dependence in earthly relationships. But even when people feel completely on top of the world, they know they are dependent on something outside themselves. They know there must be a Cause outside of themselves from which the whole of their existence derives. At the very least we owe ourselves to our parents. The cause of our abilities and capacities is not within us, but outside of us. Such intuitions of dependency are, for Schleiermacher, the primary indicators of the reality of God, who is the cause of our existence and its continuation. But "God" is therefore a function of the concept of man; starting with the religious phenomena within our existence, "God" is the name for the Origin or Ultimate Cause of these phenomena. Schleiermacher writes,

> As regards the identification of absolute dependence with "relation to God" in our proposition: this is to

be understood in the sense that the Whence of our receptive and active existence, as implied in this self-consciousness, is to be designated by the word "God," and that this is for us the really original signification of that word.... In this sense it can indeed be said that God is given to us in feeling in an original way; and if we speak of an original revelation of God to man or in man, the meaning will always be just this, that, along with the absolute dependence which characterizes not only man but all temporal existence, there is given to man also the immediate self-consciousness of it, which becomes a consciousness of God. In whatever measure this actually takes place during the course of a personality through time, in just that measure do we ascribe piety to the individual.

Thus, "God" is the religious name for the cause of our existence. God is the religious interpretation of a very secular and worldly existence. This is something like Thomas Aquinas' careful limiting of the worth of his arguments for the existence of God. Yet Aquinas denies that the first cause must be called "God," and states that such naming is only a human convention. For Aquinas, the five ways of "demonstrating" that God is, are only part of natural theology or the knowledge of God that human understanding can arrive at through independent reason, or reason unaided by revelation. But far more important than such theology is revealed theology, or what Aquinas calls "sacred doctrine." For Schleiermacher, however, at the heart of Christian faith is natural theology in the sense of what we know of God by reflecting on our emotional life; such reflection virtually eclipses revelational theology. We have a feeling of absolute dependence, a feeling that we owe ourselves to something other than ourselves. In this way we conclude we must have a "cause" external to ourselves, and this outside Cause becomes for us "God." Note the

Friedrich Daniel Ernst Schleiermacher (1768–1834)

subjectivity of Schleiermacher's logic: this Cause is, for us pious people, God. But "God" is not a necessary designation, an identity inhering in the object itself. Rather, "God" is only something in ourselves as religious or pious people, who give that name to our feeling of absolute dependency. "God" is a religious interpretation of inner experiences which can also be interpreted in other fashions, and of course will be interpreted quite differently by science. The question has always been whether "father" and "mother" cannot replace "God" in this definition. That I owe my existence not to myself can easily mean I owe it to my parents, or to my society. There have been people who claim, with every bit as much right as Schleiermacher, that this feeling of absolute dependence is to be interpreted sociologically, not theologically. That is the danger when Christianity is reduced to a set of interpretations of this-worldly or secular phenomena.

To conclude these remarks on Schleiermacher's understanding of God as our First Cause, let me state again that this is to reduce the biblical God to a general, ultimate Cause, in a timeless sense. Schleiermacher's central doctrine, that all is divine providence, does not mean God enters into the world or creates new things; God's effects are general processes. Redemption can be seen, then, only as a continuation of general creation and general providence. It is wrong to understand God in terms of God's specific acts, such as in bringing Israel through the Red Sea, or in the birth, death and resurrection of Christ. God is not known through concrete experience, but through humanity's general experience of being dependent. What Schleiermacher gives us is a fading idea of God, an impersonal deity, clearly not the intimate and almighty God who dwells in whirlwinds and counts hairs, who speaks and to whom we can speak. Schleiermacher goes to great length to demolish the idea of a personal God. To ascribe to God mercy and kindness—or any "human" feeling—is far too anthropomorphic. Such ascriptions make our understanding of God impure. God is the utterly removed Cause of everything. He is in fact, despite Schleiermacher's denials, a Platonic god.

God is the Cause of all that takes place. But He is never to be understood as a separate cause of any event. His causality is general. God is the co-determinant of events, but not the immediate cause of any event. Schleiermacher's theology diminishes God's interaction with the world to almost nothing. Indeed, for Schleiermacher, the apologetically perfect situation would be if God did not act at all, for a merely universal God would keep the idea of God kept safe from an attack by science. According to Schleiermacher, then,

> Any possibility of God being in any way given is entirely excluded, because anything that is outwardly given must be given as an object exposed to our counter-influence, however slight this may be. The transference of the idea of God to any perceptible object, unless one is all the time conscious that it is a piece of purely arbitrary symbolism, is always a corruption, whether it be a temporary transference, i.e., a theophany, or a constitutive transference, in which God is represented as permanently a particular perceptible existence.

In other words, if we declare that Jesus Christ was and is divine, or that God is the creator or the effector of any event in history, we rob him of his status as the unchangeable God. To claim that God is in some way perceptible is, Schleiermacher says, always a corruption of the very idea of God: "All attributes which we ascribe to God are to be taken as denoting not something special in God, but only something special in the manner in which the feeling of absolute dependence is to be related to Him." Here we find, strangely enough, a link between Schleiermacher and his supposed arch-enemies, the dialectical theologians of the twentieth century. For Schleiermacher has expressed here the central idea of dialectical theology: God is essentially imperceptible. Of course, Schleiermacher allows talk of God in mythological terms, as long as it understands itself to be mythological. We can speak of God acting, but must keep in mind that we use purely symbolic language. Hence there is no possibility of any real "theophany" or manifestation of God in time. In fact, any talk of God's perceptible existence is ruled out as a corruption. The question is, by what standard is such talk of God to be judged a corruption? To talk of a God who acts or does is certainly no corruption of the Christian concept of God. No, rather it is a corruption of the Platonic concept of God, which stands at every point behind Schleiermacher's doctrine of God.

(b) *Christology*. The same problems arise in Schleiermacher's christology. Because of the evolutionary nature of Schleiermacher's theological thought, he preferred to see Christ as the second Adam. Christ is truly man because of his perfect consciousness of God. There is in an ambiguity in the language here—and Schleiermacher employs ambiguity masterfully. A possessive construction is used that makes it unclear in what way Christ has the consciousness of God. Is it a consciousness of being God? Is it a consciousness of God's presence? The interpretation of Christ's God-consciousness is left entirely open—orthodox, liberal, whatever. We need to notice also the term "perfect." Basically, this measures consciousness of God in quantitative terms. Christ has no essential difference from humanity: he is perfected humanity. He represents a new creation, but only in the sense that he marks a higher spiritual development of humanity. Schleiermacher's spirituality, then, is also evolutionary. Christ, though, is unique in his power for his believers. He is not only our example of Christian living, but our power for it, too: his strength flows to us today. Since he was the founder of the church, he still inspires the church. Like God, therefore, Christ is a cause—the cause of the existing church.

Schleiermacher also speaks of Christ's ongoing and present influence in his community. For example, if a person goes from a feeling of spiritual emptiness to a feeling of spiritual strength and steadfastness, Christ is the cause. Or if a person is irreligious and becomes religious, Christ is a cause of this change, along with whatever non-religious factors might be involved. The religious psychologists perhaps can still explain the change in secular terms, but a believer knows that such explanations are in themselves insufficient. However orthodox as this account of religious experience might at first sound, there are problems at its roots. Although here Schleiermacher appears to be acknowledging Christ's divinity, this may not be the case at all. There are many other figures in world and religious history—Muhammad, Buddha, Plato—who are neither divine nor still living and yet who also exercise influence, and often spiritual influence, today. So Christ's influence over the thinking and acting of people may not be unique. Schleiermacher points out that Christ's influence is of a double nature: he is an example to emulate, and he is the first representative of a new creation. Yet, to be either or both does not require that Christ be divine.

Another problem with Schleiermacher's christology is that its truth does not require that Christ even actually existed in history. Indeed, to think that he did might create the wrong impression for people, as if it were somehow important that Christ has existence apart from their faith. Rather, all that is important, according to Schleiermacher, is the contemporary effect Christ has on the believer, particularly on the believer's feelings. Schleiermacher would perhaps disown altogether the question of whether Christ was a historic figure, and consider this question to lead only to misunderstandings and false conclusions.

(c) *The concepts of sin and salvation.* What about sin? Schleiermacher defines sin as "an arrestment of the determinative power of the spirit, due to the independence of the sensuous functions." This means that sin is a lack of religious feeling. Sin is the deviation of the life of the senses away from the life of the spirit. We see here Schleiermacher's involvement with idealism, where sin is understood to dwell in the senses, not in the mind and heart. Sin is not a willed rebellion against God, but a kind of weakness. Indeed, Schleiermacher holds to the tradition that sees evil simply as the absence of good. Perhaps he is correct in his belief that this definition of sin can be reconciled with the notion of sin as a turning away from the Creator, but this definition cannot be reconciled with the idea of sin as transgression of the Divine law. Schleiermacher solves this problem by sidestepping it: law, he says, isn't an originally Christian concept anyway. In this way, sin becomes the momentary inability to have strong religious feelings. It is not a moral or volitional defect, but rather a defect of the human constitution. Accordingly, Schleiermacher holds God directly responsible for sin.

After all the changes that Schleiermacher has wrought in the doctrines of God, Christ and sin, what becomes of salvation? Salvation is what helps to remove obstacles to the development of a strong consciousness of God. Schleiermacher, then, sees salvation as an evolutionary process, a gradual improvement. The idea of sudden conversion is repulsive to him. Ultimately, only this understanding of salvation could be possible for him, since within his understanding of man there cannot be anything we might need to be saved from. In his theology, there is no wrath of God; any such doctrine is an insult to any decent concept of God. Equally, there is no devil: Schleiermacher says, "It is impossible to conceive how persistent evil could exist side by side with superlative insight." And there is no hell; he maintains there are at least hints in Scripture of a doctrine of universal salvation, which is a much more acceptable doctrine. When the Bible is ransacked like this, it is no wonder that salvation becomes merely a modest program for self-improvement.

CRITIQUE

The most famous philosopher of Schleiermacher's era was Georg Wilhelm Friedrich Hegel (1770–1831). It is Hegel who launches the first criticism against him, beginning with remarks in 1801 in the preface to an essay, his first publication, and later in *Faith and Knowledge,* which appears the following year. Hegel is pleased to see Schleiermacher revive interest in religion after the Enlightenment's "barren desert of rationalism." However, he notes that the content of religion according to Schleiermacher seems to be left up to the individual's emotional whim. Schleiermacher has manipulated the question of truth out of existence. Religious emotions, which have replaced truth as the touchstone of faith, are not a sturdy enough foundation for faith: emotions can lack both truthfulness and sufficient dignity. If God is only the "Whence" or source of my existence, this is nothing but extrapolations from my own subjectivity into empty space. Simply put, emotions are not sufficient—or even necessary—to determine truth. Truth and goodness are not decided on the basis of personal sentiment. Such an understanding abolishes the whole question of truth. More than that, if religion consists in feelings, such religiosity ultimately abolishes all true community: people who lack the requisite feelings are excluded. In 1821, Hegel said that if religion is defined as the feeling of absolute dependence,

Friedrich Daniel Ernst Schleiermacher (1768–1834)

"a dog would be the best Christian for it possesses this in the highest degree and lives mainly in this feeling."

Ludwig Feuerbach (1804–1872), a follower and popularizer of Hegel, levels the second major criticism of Schleiermacher. Feuerbach pioneers the argument that "God" is only a "projection" of man, or that theology is actually anthropology. It is this argument that will become foundational for both Karl Marx (1818–1883) and Sigmund Freud (1856–1939). Because Schleiermacher's theology begins with human feelings, it opens itself to Feuerbach's critique. Indeed, Feuerbach says his theory is proved by Schleiermacher's own theological method: the theologian himself claims that religion is nothing but subjectivism and has no objective content. It is painfully clear that Schleiermacher and the theologians of our century who do away with the historic element of Christianity only prepare the faith for destruction; they serve it up to its critics on a silver platter. The Feuerbach-Marxist critique of religion proves that biblical faith cannot dispense with historic realities. Believers might concur in Schleiermacher's renunciation of natural theology, but we cannot follow him in forsaking history.

Schleiermacher's Platonic dread of the blood and bones of history, his fear of scientific scorn, his zeal to maintain the Kantian separation of the phenomena investigated by science from the noumena that have to do with the transcendent God—all this is quite contrary to the Bible. The biblical God declares, "I have heard, I have seen . . . I have come down to help" (Ex. 3:7, 8). No wonder Schleiermacher discarded the Old Testament! But he also clearly has a Platonic dread of the Incarnation in the New Testament. Schleiermacher's theology reverses John 1:14—"The Word became flesh." For him, the flesh becomes word; "God" becomes merely an interpretation of man. Schleiermacher's God is a Platonic God, not the God of Scripture.

Therefore we must, against Schleiermacher, reassert that God is the God of history. Joachim Jeremias (b. 1900)—a great New Testament scholar best known for his work on the parables—once said Golgotha is not everywhere (as if Christ would die in all our hearts and rise again in us); there is only one Golgotha and it is situated outside of the gates of Jerusalem. Christianity is essentially, unavoidably historical. Some scholars have observed that there is much in common between Schleiermacher's concept of Christ in us and evangelicalism's emphasis on Christ in us. But that observation is misleading because evangelicalism always presupposes—or always should presuppose—that the historical Christ and the authority of Scripture are the norms for the experience of Christ in us. More than that, the nature and content of experience which evangelicalism describes is different from what Schleiermacher describes. Schleiermacher's consciousness of God is a very general experience. Evangelicalism and Pietism, on the other side, describe concrete, particular experiences, not general experiences in terms of providence. So there is no real common ground between Schleiermacher and evangelicalism: Schleiermacher begins with experience, evangelicalism with historical revelation. Although evangelicalism today, as I have noted previously in these lectures, seems increasingly tempted toward beginning with experience, we can still say that for evangelicals Scripture must be primary, and experience must be tested against it. The revelation of the Word always precedes feeling.

Can anything be salvaged from Schleiermacher? Karl Barth, in his otherwise very thorough trouncing of Schleiermacher, names three items which speak in his favour. First, Schleiermacher at least insists that theologians and pastors be convinced of what they preach. In the generation before Schleiermacher, preachers had to preach orthodoxy even if they didn't believe it; hence, there was a lot of

Friedrich Daniel Ernst Schleiermacher (1768–1834)

officially sanctioned hypocrisy. Second, Schleiermacher teaches that theology must serve the church and not be a pedant's game; Barth of course has a particular interest in seeing dogmatics as church dogmatics and not simply as a scholarly undertaking. Third, Schleiermacher preaches the entire length of his life, Sunday after Sunday; Schleiermacher was not the typical liberal intellectual who withdraws from the church.

Overall, we must thank Schleiermacher for his wholehearted commitment to the cultural recovery of religion after the onslaught of rationalism. Yet, like many theologians after him, Schleiermacher pursues this worthy goal on his own terms, and by doing so diminishes theology; his theological method was to diminish theology for the next 200 years. And we must note that Schleiermacher's romanticist attempt to protect religion from the rationalist critique ran straight into the psychological and the sociological critiques of religion. He sought refuge from Enlightenment rationalism in the crushing arms of Feuerbach, Marx, and Freud.

Meditation
Psalm 119:144-145

Your statutes are forever right;
  give me understanding that I may live.
I call with all my heart; answer me, O Lord,
  and I will obey your decrees.

We could follow the interesting sequence of verbs in these two verses. I am a stickler for verbs, and always look at them first in doing exegesis. Here we have a very interesting sequence of verbs, but let's look at something else. "I will obey your decrees." It clearly shows the intention of the person. The dialectical theologians were very far from this when they said the commandments couldn't be kept; only Christ kept the commandments.

His keeping of the commandments is being reckoned as our righteousness. There is almost a substitutionary keeping of the commandments. It leaves nothing for us. The double commandment of love, of God and of neighbour, needs to be the standard not only of our lives but also of all theology. It implies a dedication of the three main faculties: mind (to which the dialectical theologians also agreed), will, passions (to love God passionately). In dialectical theology, the gospel was intellectualized. It can easily mean that the will and emotions can run around and do what they want. It also means feelings and will remain outside of our dedication. It is clearly a compromise solution. It wasn't radical enough (a strange thing to say to dialectical theologians).

Meditation

It is not even radical enough in the area of Karl Barth's supreme concern. God is not supreme in the area of our will or feeling.

So I am looking for the kind of moral commitment that you see preached in Ritschl, and the passionate dedication to God on the emotional side like you see in early pietism (especially in Count Zinzendorf, the founder of the Moravian Church). Both are also found in Puritanism. At the same time, people like Ritschl and Schleiermacher are one-sided. Ritschl requires the dedication to God of the will, but in thinking, in doctrine, he is absolutely liberal and reserves the right to decide himself. In Schleiermacher, you have that commitment of the feelings. That's where God is encountered. But in terms of thought and doctrine there is not harnessing of the mind, but complete freedom. He says there's no difference between pantheism and theism. Barth is third in that triangle. Schleiermacher emphasized the feeling. Ritschl emphasized the will. Barth emphasizes the mind. Each reserves for man the right to rule the other two faculties.

The same problem is very deep in Protestantism in general with its strong emphasis on faith, with faith being the foremost virtue of the believer. I am writing a foreword to a reissue of Lütgert's (Schlatter's colleague) *Love in the New Testament* (1905). The book is completely forgotten. Even Leon Morris (the Australian exegete) is unaware of the book in his book *Love in the Bible* (1982). Such a book is easily forgotten in Protestantism. Right from the time of the Reformation, faith was seen as the proper relationship to God, not love. There are passages in Luther and Schleiermacher and Ritschl which reject the idea of love for God. It is part of the greatness of Karl Barth that in his old age he admitted that there is love of God in Scripture, and therefore it is appropriate to love God, and not only believe God.

Psalm 119:44–45

The problem here is the term "faith." You can claim that faith contains all of the other things, and see love of God as a part of it (Melanchthon, in his commentary on the Augsburg Confession, says they are not to be accused of not having good works, because when they speak of faith they mean faith associated with good works). We can give any theological term our own content. But when it is not part of the actual meaning of the word we make it very difficult for people to know what we mean. What we have here is a synecdochical understanding of faith. (Recall that famous method of interpreting the Ten Commandments, where the negative command implies the positive, and vice versa, i.e., Calvin's "To each prohibition corresponds a command.") I do not trust the power of synecdoche. It is not guaranteed that everyone who hears the term "faith" will immediately say, "That is the beautiful trust and confidence of which love is a part and from which good works follow." Love of God is not intrinsic in the word "faith." It should not be claimed that everybody understands that without it being made explicit. That's what we have in dialectical theology. Dialectical theology turned the keeping of the commandments into the non-keeping of the commandments. The keeping of the commandments is reserved for Christ. We are being reckoned righteous because he kept the commandments. Their argument is that if we try to keep the commandments, we take honour from Christ.

You can be as theological as you want, but step by step you must examine the results of your theologizing against Scripture. Here the psalm says, "I will keep your commandments." I will not rely on the fact that they have already been kept for me. That may be true, but it does not make keeping them myself superfluous. The keeping of the commandments has not become redundant by Christ's perfect obedience.

Chapter Two

LIBERALISM WITHIN THE CHURCH: ALBRECHT RITSCHL (1822–1889)

There are two kinds of liberal theologians. One is radical; they usually end up leaving the church and denying the specifics of Christianity. A representative figure is David Friedrich Strauss (1808–1874), the famous—or, for Barth, "infamously famous"—author of *Life of Jesus Critically Examined* (1835). The other kind of liberal theologian stays inside the church. Schleiermacher was our first representative here. His was a churchly and devout liberalism. The same can be said of Adolf von Harnack. In him, we meet a dogmatic liberal who is at the same time absolutely devout. Albrecht Ritschl is also a prominent representative of this kind of theologian. He is therefore the link between Schleiermacher and the twentieth century. Harnack was Ritschl's star student, so we will look at the two side-by-side.

RITSCHL'S LIFE

Albrecht Ritschl (1822–1889) was the son of a conservative pastor who later became a bishop. There is, it appears, a common trend here: leading liberals are often the children of either evangelicals or orthodox (Harnack and Karl Barth—who didn't remain a liberal—were also both sons of Reformational orthodox or evangelical parents). Ritschl is typical in this respect. He wanted, like his father, to serve in the church, and so studied theology. He went to the rather conservative faculty of Bonn for his studies. But he was disturbed by the false intellectual tranquility of the place. "Inside," he said of Bonn, "a harmony prevails which is nowhere existent outside." No one was wrestling with culture's dominant ideas. Ritschl was annoyed by the lack of antithesis and struggle in the work of Bonn's professors. The question which haunts us here is whether this is true, not just then but today, of many conservative faculties.

After Bonn, Ritschl went to the other conservative university, Halle. This was the evangelical school. August Tholuck, the very prominent leader of the theological revival in the first half of the nineteenth century, was teaching at Halle at the time. He had almost single-handedly wiped out the remnant of rationalism in the faculty of Halle. Tholuck then developed Halle as the centre of evangelical or revival theology, and Ritschl became his student. Tholuck has been called the "Father of Students." There were hundreds of pastors who derived their faith and commitment from the years they studied with him. Ritschl developed a personal contact with Tholuck that lasted a lifetime. After Ritschl became a famous professor, he would visit Tholuck summer after summer, even though his old professor and mentor didn't have much sympathy for Ritschl's theological stance. Ritschl reported, to his amazement, that old Tholuck would press him about his personal faith. Unfortunately, though, Tholuck had no lasting theological influence on Ritschl. Writing home to his father, Ritschl said, "Tholuck is an unsystematic genius. His lectures in exegesis, early on in the term, are getting sloppy. There's no systematic discipline here. Tholuck moves about with too many students to be in depth with a few." (Again, is that typical of evangelicals?) "There is more poetry and more piety in him than theology. The only consistent thing is him himself in his subjectivity. That clearly is characteristic, of course, but it is not sufficient for theology."

But Ritschl did take one inheritance from Tholuck. He took Tholuck's great theme of reconciliation. He had heard Tholuck describe reconciliation as "a theme for the future." Tholuck himself had recovered the topic of reconciliation after the time of Schleiermacher. There was no room for reconciliation in Schleiermacher's theology because he saw sin not as hostility but only as weakness. Yet Ritschl, in developing the theme of reconciliation, did not follow evangelical convictions, but rather began with a book on the history of reconciliation by a theologian at Tübingen, the historian of dogma F. C. Baur (1792–1860).

Interestingly enough, it was Tholuck himself who drew Ritschl's attention to Baur's work; in a sense he sent Ritschl into the liberal camp, for Tübingen was extremely liberal at the time, and Baur especially so. Baur constructed history on the basis of Hegelian dialectic, in which one idea (thesis) comes in conflict with another (an antithesis), which together lead to a better, third idea (the resulting synthesis). So Christianity becomes the synthesis of Judaism and its antithesis Hellenism. On such a scheme, the whole idea of revelation is excluded. Each thesis is already a synthesis of earlier antitheses. This is a clumsy way of doing history, and insensitive. But it can be successful, and has a beauty of its own: it is basically a mental construction, and the hard awkward facts of real history need not intrude. Ritschl's first book, in which he argued that Luke was written after pro-Pauline champion Marcion (2nd century), was an academic failure, refuted by all his colleagues. As a result, he turned to a less synthetic history of dogma, returned to philosophically unprejudiced research, and became even rather conservative as an historian, even thinking that Ephesians and Colossians were actually written by Paul himself.

At age 24, Ritschl became a university lecturer. But these were years of waiting: it took thirteen years after completing his doctorate to finally become a full professor. He married the same year—at age 37. At the time, you couldn't marry until you became a professor (even in 1960 the expectation in Germany was that you didn't marry until tenured). Once a full professor at Göttingen, he began to write his major works. *History of the Doctrine of Reconciliation* is the most famous (the third volume, *Christian Doctrine of Justification and Reconciliation*, is his own dogmatics). "Christian Perfection" is a pamphlet which he wrote for the ladies of the faculty. It is a speech intended to introduce them to his main work. He also wrote *Three Essays*, intended to be used as religious instruction for high school students—but far too difficult for that level.

Ritschl abhorred pietists. He saw, to his disgust, a number of evangelicals at that time (the students of Halle, for instance) engaged in power politics in the church. Wanting to banish pietism as an active force in the church, he wrote his three-volume *History of Pietism*. This was meant to show the impossibility of holding to pietistic ideals. At the time, liberals thought the best weapon against an enemy was to look into their history, since everyone has skeletons in the closet. The "Introduction" to the *History of Pietism*, which reveals Ritschl's prejudices, has been translated in the *Three Essays*. Most of Ritschl's fame came through his students. He lived to see the appointment of Harnack. His wife died after only ten years of marriage, and he took it in a stoic fashion. He educated his children, never remarried, and died himself at age 67.

Liberalism Within the Church: Albrecht Ritschl

RITSCHL'S THEOLOGY

Prolegomena
Theology begins with prolegomena—"things which need to be said first." These include things such as reason and revelation, natural theology, and the sources of theological knowledge. Ritschl's prolegomena are quite new. They begin with the matter-of-fact presupposition of Kant's critique. Ritschl is the Kantian theologian of the nineteenth century. His theology, both in what he affirms and what he denies, is Kantian. There is no room for any natural theology, or any discussion of the proofs for the existence of God, which are the traditional starting points for theology. The starting point is not history, metaphysics nor personal experience (as in Schleiermacher). The starting point, rather, is the existing church and its faith as a witness to God.

This can't be debated. The church is there. Ritschl's theology is statistical (as in Schleiermacher), but Ritschl measures the faith of the church, not of the individual. If Schleiermacher's approach was subjectivism, Ritschl's is objectivism. Between Schleiermacher and Ritschl stood a century of religious subjectivity. There was Schleiermacher with all his pupils; pietist theology, which was very subjective; and the Lutherans, especially Franz Hermann Reinhold von Frank (1827–1894) at the influential University of Erlangen, who expressly said we have to begin theology with a personal experience of God. One of these theologians codified this starting point in a startling phrase: "I, the Christian, am to me the theologian, the only object of science." So the theologian studies the self, the self's religious feelings, and describes those as the contents of dogmatics. Dogmatics had become highly subjective. Ritschl, however, excluded religious subjectivity from theology.

And in this, he has shaped the last hundred years of theology. Ritschl's prolegomena is all about the church;

the church is the source of theology. The church is the fundament. Ritschl's dogmatics is very much a "church dogmatics" (to use Barth's phrase). The church's faith is always prior to the faith of the individual (this is another antipietistic pronouncement). The church, not the individual, is the object of salvation. The individual's faith is always communicated and mediated by the church. Ritschl does away with Schleiermacher and subjectivity with a single sentence: "One doesn't look into oneself for certainty, but trusts the message of the church." Even the language—"one doesn't"—is impersonal. His critics accused him of a Roman concept of the church, claiming that he was saying the same thing as "outside of the church there is no salvation."

Ethics in Ritschl's Theology

In Ritschl's theology, ethics are also pre-eminent. Here the whole Kantian formation of his theology comes to the fore. The Christian stance is ethical. With relish, Ritschl and all his pupils quote John 7:17: "If anyone chooses to do God's will, he will find out whether my teaching comes from God or whether I speak on my own."

It is not emotions (pointing to the pietists and the Schleiermacher camp) which render Christ's teaching true, but doing God's will, living the Christian life. At the core of Ritschl's theology is ethics, which has been called his "moralism."

Yet in Ritschl there is hardly any emphasis on the individual and therefore very little (if any) on a personal relationship with God. Ritschl's God is not a personal God but a God of providence, remote from human affairs. Ritschl criticizes evangelicalism or pietism as "chumminess" with Jesus. We are not to see ourselves as the friends of Jesus. Rather, we should see ourselves as servants of the Lord. Ritschl saw pietism as a descendent of medieval Roman

Liberalism Within the Church: Albrecht Ritschl

Catholic mysticism and as such having no room in the Reformational Protestant church.

Ritschl described his ideal of the Christian life as follows: (1) trusting in God's providence; (2) resigning oneself to faith; (3) learning to humbly listen to one's fate (Ritschl's concept of divine guidance) and having an open ear to circumstances; (4) having courage and freedom from human prejudice, especially in religion (this fourth condition is the stance of the liberal who does not believe in orthodox authority; his liberalism emerges strongly here: he basically denies the church's precedents and traditions and exalts independence); and (5) practicing daily prayer.

All of this is human action, which is one of the basic problems in Ritschl's theology. This is clearly evident, for example, in Ritschl's understanding of reconciliation. For him, peace with God is gained through human action. "Reconciliation," he said, "is experienced in active trust in God's providence." Those who actively trust in God's providence—not in the saving work of Christ—can know that they are reconciled with God.

Vocation in Ritschl's Ethics

Vocation is another emphasis in Ritschl's concept of the Christian life. Here, he describes the ideal in terms derived from the Reformers' description of Christian perfection. In the Augsburg Confession, Article 27, Melanchthon says— in opposition to the monastic concept of perfection—that "True Christian perfection consists of prayer for our needs, expecting and trusting in God's help in affliction, in our calling and station in life, and doing good works and attending to our vocation." The concept of vocation comes up twice in this short text. Ritschl agreed with this. For him, as much as for the Reformers, the Christian life is lived out primarily in one's civil vocation. That is where the decisive things happen.

The Kingdom of God as an Ethical Category

Another important item in Ritschl's theology is the recovery of the concept of the kingdom of God. And here again we see the preeminence of ethics for him. Protestant theology up until the time of Ritschl had almost eclipsed talk of the kingdom of God. This was Ritschl's innovation. But he not only recovered the idea of the kingdom of God, he also turned it into an ethical—rather than a dogmatic—category. The kingdom is man's activity, not God's.

Ritschl said theology as a science is elliptical: it has two foci. We should not orient theology, as we have in the past, around only one focus. Since the Reformation, theologians have been playing the game of trying to find the centre of Scripture.

Luther said the centre was justification, with Romans and Galatians at the heart. Then came Corinthians and John, and then the synoptic gospels. And then on the outside—where the air gets chilly—was the letter of James. Theologians continue to play this game today, to search for a single centre. It gives them an opportunity to present their own preferred doctrines. But Ritschl shrewdly said there were two centres: the sonship of the Christian (we are reconciled children of God) and the kingdom of God. His two centres are soteriology and the kingdom. In the first focus, God is, hopefully, the agent (though, as we've seen, Ritschl had a human-centred understanding of this doctrine). But in the second focus, the kingdom, man is clearly the agent, making it not a dogmatic focus but an ethical one.

What are the implications of the kingdom of God being introduced for the first time as an ethical category? To answer that, we need to set Ritschl's view against a traditional understanding of the kingdom of God. Traditionally, there are two main interpretations of the kingdom of God. The first is the psychological understanding: the kingdom of God is identified with faith. This was the position, for example, of Luther and Melanchthon. The kingdom of God is in the soul of each believer. It is within the believer, and so hidden. This interpretation is based on Luke 17:21, which says the kingdom of God is *entos humon*. The phrase can be translated either "within you" or "among you."

The second interpretation of the kingdom of God is the eschatological. The kingdom of God is something that will come at the end of the world. It is not so much within as beyond, a transcendent reality.

Ritschl, against both interpretations, says that the kingdom of God is moral. The kingdom of God is the product of the church. It is not so much a divine gift, but a moral and spiritual task of humanity assembled in the church. This interpretation of the kingdom of God again lands him squarely within the Kantian framework. In the last analysis, Ritschl describes the kingdom of God as humanity's civilizing effort.

There is a strong and admirable concern for culture and society here. But note: this is not really a concern for social justice. It is, rather, a concern for culture from the standpoint of the educated middle and upper-middle class. Schleiermacher, with his philosophical idealism, would feel comfortable here—in this realm where the human spirit is in a constant struggle to overcome the crude forces of nature and human nature. This is the ideal of the Greek god Apollo: order versus chaos. Culture is the humanizing of nature. This is what Ritschl understood as the kingdom of God. God is hidden behind his kingdom, eclipsed by the efforts of men. It is a kingdom where the King doesn't have very much to say. Half a century later, Ritschl's understanding of the kingdom of God came to fruition in Walter Rauschenbusch's social gospel.

As mentioned earlier, Ritschl viewed the kingdom of God as realized in one's civil vocation. Civil vocation is the field of Christian existence. This is yet another polemic against pietism, with its continuation of medieval asceticism and religious activities. Ritschl saw pietism, with its roots in medieval theology, as alienated from the concerns of culture. There is no need to go to China to preach the gospel, but only this: love your neighbor and fulfil your civil vocation. So Ritschl was strongly opposed to the great pietistic missionary movement of his time. The command, he said, was to "love your neighbor," not foreign strangers. He urged Christians, in obedience to the kingdom ethic, to stay home and fulfil their civil vocation.

Ritschl's Christology

Ritschl's doctrine of civil vocation is so central that it even determines his doctrine of Christ. That is why we have discussed his ethical stance before his dogmatics. Ritschl, following up on an idea present in Schleiermacher's theology, understands Christ from his work. Any person, he argues, is understood from his work, and not only his work, but his work in terms of vocation.

Extending this idea, Ritschl claimed that vocation becomes central to Christology. How so? Christ's vocation was to introduce to the world the idea of a moral kingdom of God. Christ lived his life in perfect obedience to this task, this vocation. Proclaiming the kingdom of God was Christ's life work. His death on the cross was the seal on his obedience, and "the summary of his valuable life in the service of God."

But what about the divinity of Christ? Christ was the "revealer of God" (note the ambiguous genitive "of," similar to what we saw in Schleiermacher). This can mean Christ is God; but it can alternately mean that he was just a man and only revealed God in a prophetic fashion. Ritschl means that God's nature—his love, mercy and justice—came to the fore in Christ's actions. In a less veiled manner he says divinity is a moral predicate. Divinity is not to be understood as unity of nature between Father and Son, but a unity of will—which Christ fulfilled by his fidelity to his calling. For Ritschl, to say Christ is God is not an ontological statement but a moral predicate. This is the church's value judgment, given to describe the perfection of Christ's obedience. We call him divine because he is of uttermost value to us. In Kantian terminology, to say that Christ is divine is a synthetic judgment, not an analytical one. (An analytical judgment is based on something within the subject. With a synthetic judgment, however, something is added to the subject in the moment of making the judgment.) Ritschl treats the resurrection of Christ similarly. That Christ rose from the dead is a predicate which the church avers. By this claim, we declare that Christ's sacrifice was not in vain. The doctrine of the resurrection means that Christ's purpose—but not his person—lives on. His convictions live on. His purpose of announcing the kingdom of God to the world continues. We will meet this thinking again in the Bultmann school.

Other Topics in Ritschl's Theology

What about Ritschl's conception of God? Ritschl himself saw the doctrine of God as the core of faith. Theological schools, he declared, are characterized by their idea of God. So what of Ritschl's idea of God? For him, God is the remote God of providence. Divine guidance comes through our circumstances, which we must humbly accept. We are but servants of God, not his friends, not his children. God is so remote that prayer, rather than being an act of intimate speech, of speaking and listening, is only an act of thanksgiving and of resignation to one's situation.

What does this do to petitionary prayer? Ritschl said it is presumptuous to make petitions. It is sheer arrogance to think that, for our little purposes, we can move the hand of the Creator by our praying.

We glimpse Schleiermacher sitting in the shadows of some of Ritschl's other theological ideas. Like Schleiermacher, Ritschl expressly removed the idea of the wrath of God from theology. He also, like Schleiermacher, rejected the concept of original sin as an impossible notion. He understood eschatology in terms of eternal life now—eternal life being not a future quantity, but a quality of life now. And salvation? The traditional order of salvation (something like: calling, illumination, justification, regeneration, sanctification; no two theologians have the same order) Ritschl simplified to infant baptism alone: at that moment, he said, all those other things take place. He dismissed the traditional order of salvation with the epithet "methodism."

Critique

Four general considerations enter into our critique of Ritschl's theology. First, compared with Schleiermacher, Ritschl's theology is Kant *redivivus*, with religion strongly linked to ethics. For the most part, that is a welcome recovery. It is a good corrective to some forms of Calvinist and Lutheran theology. Ritschl speaks at this point to the neglect of and the disrespect for the task of sanctification which is often evident in Lutheranism. Those Calvinists who were John Wesley's enemies were of the same type—antinomians. There is, in fact, an antinomian strain which runs right through all Protestantism. Against this, Ritschl says that Christianity has a moral backbone. Religion is not linked to emotions or mere thought systems; it is linked to ethics. Even the emphasis on Christ as a moral teacher is, in this respect, good. Ritschl is the great Kantian in modern theology, taking a rare stance for moral uprightness and seriousness.

However necessary, moral uprightness and seriousness are an insufficient sign of the Christian faith. A merely moral person could also be stoic. And, in fact, there is more than one similarity in Ritschl's theology to stoicism. The whole emphasis on the God of providence is very stoical. In Ritschl, the gospel is not only linked to ethics, but is basically *reduced* to ethics. Ritschl's theology can be criticized, and has been, as a reversal of the gospel into law.

Second, Christian ethics is reduced to civil decency, to probity—that is, virtue or integrity tested and confirmed; strict honesty. Ethics has nothing to do with piety. This is the traditional Reformational ethics of sustainment: the creational ethos. And Ritschl, like the Reformers, gives little thought to the other area of Christian ethics, the ethics of restoration, of healing. Sin causes brokenness—in hearts, souls, families, creation—and we need an ethic that acknowledges this and does something about it. But that is missing in Ritschl. He understands almost nothing of charity outside the family, and there is no place in his theology for the task of missions.

Charity and missions were of course the tenets of pietism and monasticism, and Ritschl denounced both. Pietism was right in its recovery of these works of extra-mural charity and missions which were lacking in the Protestant Reformation, with its emphasis on staying in one's vocation in life. Ritschl recovered the Reformational attitude, and by that recovery lost a theology for those peculiarly Christian works.

Third, Ritschl's christology is reductionistic and meager. His claim that christological statements are value judgments of the church and not factual, ontological statements is, at the very least, problematic. There is an interpretational problem here. The church, in fact, does make ontological statements: for example, "God was in Christ." This is not the language of value judgment.

When Ritschl calls them value judgments, he has already reinterpreted them. But worse, in turning the ontological statements into value judgments instead of statements of fact, Ritschl has submitted to the strictures of rationalism. Rationalism, not Christianity, disallows ontological statements.

Worse still, when he turns ontological statements into value judgments he unwittingly makes all of theology subjective. Only, instead of people making value judgments, it is the church which makes them. We are back to subjectivism, only this time it is a collective subjectivism, instead of an individual kind as in Schleiermacher.

Our fourth and last criticism of Ritschl is the most serious. Ritschl, by his reduction of ontological statements into value judgments, delivers Christianity on a silver platter to his contemporary Ludwig Feuerbach (1804–1872), the man whose criticism of religion both Karl Marx and Sigmund Freud embraced. Feuerbach's system is exactly this: he criticizes religion as subjectivism.

All religion is, he claims, anthropocentric. Whether an individual anthropocentrism as in Schleiermacher or a collective church anthropocentrism as in Ritschl, it doesn't make much difference: both fall easy prey to Feuerbach's criticism. Feuerbach says that there is no factual basis to religion. Rather, all religions are mere composites of value judgments and subjectivism. God, Christ—these are nothing more than projections of moral and aesthetic values; they are human values projected onto divine persons. So Ritschl's stance, despite some strengths, leaves him in desperate peril. He is as vulnerable as Schleiermacher. Feuerbach wrote a monograph showing how his criticism of Christianity was particularly apt with respect to the theology of Schleiermacher; Schleiermacher had done just what Feuerbach would have wanted in preparing Christianity for the death blow. Ritschl is not much different. What looked like objectivism at the beginning turned out to be a collective subjectivism.

Liberalism Within the Church: Albrecht Ritschl

THE THEOLOGICAL SCHOOL OF RITSCHLIANISM

Theology as Strategy

Ritschl, in the battle to establish his views, believed that doing theology was the best strategy. There was, in the beginning of the nineteenth century, a vast religious revival going on, of which Tholuck was the representative theologian. But by 1850 many of Tholuck's students had abandoned evangelicalism and turned toward Lutheran confessionalism. Many of the remaining evangelicals, and especially these young orthodox people, moved into church politics rather than theology. Tholuck had no successor. So when Ritschl appeared on the scene, evangelicalism lacked representation in the universities. They had all moved into positions of church leadership. Ritschl took the opposite approach. He was invited into church government several times, but always declined: he saw that the formation of future leaders was decisive in shaping the theological future, and so stayed in the university. Ritschl wrote to his young pupil Harnack to trust God, keep the gunpowder dry, and write the textbooks of theology. From our historical perspective we can see that this was the Jesuit model, the same formula used in the Counter Reformation: teach and print. That was how the Counter Reformation was successful in the southern half of Germany, Italy and France.

The strategy worked. Ritschl appealed to the bright, young men of the day. Why? First, he had a powerful systematic. He had been, we saw, disappointed by the lack of systematic thought in Tholuck. Evangelicals in general lacked this. There was among evangelicals a scorn for reason. Ritschl redressed this imbalance.

Second, Ritschl's position was, nevertheless, middle of the road: liberalism within the church, as opposed to Strauss (who was thrown out of the church) and to the non-theologizing evangelicals.

Third, Ritschl's theology was also marvelously open to culture (in contrast to dead orthodoxy and the evangelicals who were alienated from culture and who had no idea about what was going on in literature, in theatre, in science). They called the evangelicals *Kulturmuffel*, cultural sticks-in-the-mud. The evangelicals posed as a counter-culture, but not in the proper moral sense of the term. Ritschl, in contrast, celebrated the accomplishments of culture.

Fourth, nothing succeeds like success. There was an enormous euphoria among these young people. They were "with it," on the offensive. It was exhilarating to be in the fast lane, both theologically and in terms of academic careers. "How wonderful to be alive," wrote Ritschl.

Ritschl's Pupils

None of Ritschl's pupils studied with him at Göttingen; they only read his books. "Teach and print": the strategy worked well indeed. Wilhelm Herrmann (1846–1922) was Tholuck's teaching assistant and Ritschl's most famous student. Tholuck, in old age, said to Herrmann, "I can't do anything for you," and sent him to Ritschl. Unfortunately, Herrmann turned into a liberal studying under Ritschl. Some of Ritschl's other pupils were Johannes Weiss (1863–1914), Julius Kaftan (1848–1926), Schürer (Old Testament), Fredrich Loofs (history of doctrine), Gottshick and Kattenbusch (practical theology), and others. These were all important people around the turn of the century. From 1875 this group published the most important theological journal of the twentieth century, *Theologische Literaturzeitung*. It consists entirely of book reviews (German, French, Italian, English). The reviews were all done from the mindset of the Ritschlian school, and they were scathing. The publication of this magazine was a monthly bloodbath for other theologians, a real regime of terror. Ten years later they added a weekly magazine for educated laity (where

Liberalism Within the Church: Albrecht Ritschl

Barth started as an editorial assistant). They reviewed Adolf Schlatter's first book and butchered it. Sales abruptly stopped. The success of Ritschl's school carries us right into the twentieth century, the main concern of this book.

Meditation
PSALM 119:167–168

I obey your statutes,
 for I love them greatly.
I obey your precepts and your statutes,
 for all my ways are known to you.

Submit all your plans to God. Make plans and submit them to the Lord. Enter alliances if necessary on the condition that the Lord affirms them. And wait for the direction of his Spirit. As we have seen before in the previous meditation on Psalm 119, there is the search for individual direction and the keeping of the commandments, and even loving God's commandments. There is no contradiction in Scripture between norm and situation. This antithesis has fuelled a major debate in ethics in the past twenty years. If you go right through Scripture, the phrase "keeping the commandments" has a surprisingly prominent role, even in Paul and Revelation. It is not something which is left behind when we have understood grace. The curse on the trespassing of the commandments has been removed but the commandments themselves remain valid, even when you've found a new source of motivation. We need to remind ourselves of this in a century and a generation which has seen a general trend towards the other side, antinomianism.

Chapter Three

THE POST-RITSCHL LIBERAL SCHOOL: JOHANNES WEISS AND ADOLF VON HARNACK

In the last chapter, we looked at the pinnacle of liberal theology at the end of the nineteenth century: Albrecht Ritschl. In this chapter we will look at some other highlights through the whole course of that century. First, we will look at the fate of the liberal school following Ritschl.

JOHANNES WEISS (1863–1914)

Johannes Weiss was Ritschl's son-in-law. Also the son of the famous conservative New Testament scholar Bernhard Weiss (1827–1918), he died in the first days of World War I. Johannes Weiss was in some ways early thunder and lightning for the Ritschlian school. He was a professor of New Testament at Göttingen, Marburg, and Heidelberg. His most famous book is *Jesus' Proclamation of the Kingdom of God*, published in 1892 (gracefully after the death of his father-in-law, Ritschl). There was an expanded second edition in 1900. The English translation (Fortress Press,

1971) has an extensive introduction with biographical information. Weiss, who was one of Bultmann's teachers, demolished exegetically the theology of his father-in-law Ritschl because he demonstrated the gap between Jesus' eschatological concept of the kingdom of God and Ritschl's ethical idea of the kingdom of God. Weiss demythologized Ritschl's concept of the kingdom of God, which saw the kingdom as the exercise of the moral life in society and the gradual realization of a moral ideal on earth. Weiss, in sharp contrast, said the kingdom of God in the New Testament is completely eschatological and apocalyptic, needing to be understood as analogous to Jewish apocalypticism. There are at least four points which are important in understanding the kingdom of God in the New Testament and the message of Jesus: (1) It is transcendental, otherworldly. It comes down from heaven, rather than being built on earth towards heaven. (2) It is not present but will come down in the future. (3) It clearly is not evolutionary but will come down suddenly and complete. (4) It is God's deed, a gift not a task. It is nothing but grace. Therefore one cannot say Jesus founded the kingdom of God (as Ritschl had put it); rather, Christ expected it. In summary, "The kingdom of God as Jesus thought of it is never something subjective, inward, or spiritual. But it is always the objective messianic kingdom which is pictured as a treasure which comes down from heaven." So the kingdom of God in the New Testament is something completely different from that central concept in Ritschl's theology.

What consequences arise from this? What shall we do now? Weiss answered that we must continue to use kingdom of God language, but knowing we do so in a way different from Jesus. In choosing between the alternative concepts of Jesus and Ritschl, of course we have to choose Ritschl. We don't, Weiss said, have Christ's eschatological expectations any more. On the contrary, Ritschl is theologically correct even if he is exegetically wrong. The conclusion of the book reads as follows:

> The difference between our modern Protestant worldview and that of primitive Christianity is that we do not share their eschatological attitude. Namely, this world is no longer passing away for us (cf. 1 Cor. 7:31). We no longer pray, "May grace come and may the world pass away." We pass our lives in the joyful confidence that this world will evermore be the show place of the people of God.

Here we see Weiss's subscription to the evolutionary concept of the kingdom of God. According to Weiss, among ourselves the New Testament eschatological attitude can only be approximated by our own approaching death, with the respective ethos: live as if you were dying tomorrow. The future eschatology of the kingdom is reduced to a present day eschatology of one's own approaching death. We saw this replacement of future eschatology with present day eschatology in Schleiermacher. Eschatology means "last things" not in the sense of the last things in time, but of the things of ultimate importance. It is no longer a quantitative concept, but qualitative. This is the understanding of eschatology we encounter also in the Bultmann school. Johannes Weiss is the link between Schleiermacher's invention of the reduction of eschatology and the contemporary Bultmann school.

ADOLF VON HARNACK (1851–1930)

Harnack is the Ritschlian crown prince, the star of the school. In 1914 he was made a baron (and so dubbed "von"). He was the son of Theodosios Harnack, a strictly orthodox Lutheran, who taught at Dorpat in Estonia. Theodosios produced two volumes on Luther's theology in which he stressed that God, not man, does the essential things. This was clearly an orthodox position with a strongly anti-liberal bent. The work was actually republished in the 1920s by the leading men in the dialectical movement. This, then—a strictly Lutheran orthodox home, a father who was a leading exponent of Lutheran orthodoxy—was the background of this prominent liberal.

Adolf von Harnack was a brilliant young man. At 23, he was already a lecturer in church history at the University of Leipzig—the seat of Lutheran orthodoxy. So he began within his father's fold. But through reading the theological literature of the day, he joined the Ritschlian school. What did Harnack find in Ritschl that the orthodox Lutherans couldn't give him? He said, "It was a bright and optimistic theology. Christianity must not load us down with additional riddles." More than that, this was liberalism within the church. He could be both Enlightened and a churchman.

For Harnack, Ritschl's theology was a return to rationality, and stood in sharp contrast to the somberness of orthodox Lutheran theology. It was a theology built on not dogmatism, but the simple religion of Jesus himself: "A child-like religion, confidence in God as Father, living with Christ." One believes not in Christ, but like Christ. This is the usual liberal understanding of Jesus as the exemplar of faith.

At age 24, Harnack was made a full professor at Giessen; he then moved on to neighboring Marburg. His career took off like a rocket. He wrote, "Minds are waking everywhere." And then, echoing Ritschl, "How glorious to be alive!" There was a new springtime for theology in the offing. But it was not, Harnack saw, a time for resting. Diligence was the watchword. "Teach and preach." His field was the history of doctrine, especially of the early church. Before age 30, he had published the magnificent three-volume (seven volumes in the English translation) *The History of Dogma*. This was state-of-the-art theology, a paradigm of theology in his generation. The product of a cultured, erudite, theological historian who at the same time was a brilliant writer makes for inspiring reading.

Later, when Harnack was involved in a theological quarrel with somebody, he revealed the motive behind his diligent historical work: "You must counter the errors of the day with a large mass of history." *The History of Dogma* became famous because it was written from one central concept, the early Hellenization of Christianity and of doctrine. As a result of this early success, Harnack in 1888 was chosen as professor of history of doctrine at Berlin, the capital of the new empire (1871). This was the most prominent academic position available. His election caused an uproar in the church, and there was a tremendous controversy in the newspapers and magazines because the orthodox and conservative people in church government contested the election. But, as happens so often, the orthodox and conservatives had no alternative candidate ready to present. So they were silenced. The whole academic community went outdoors as a show of strong support for Harnack.

Marburg, where Harnack was teaching, quickly made him rector of the university—a strategic move to defend Harnack from his critics, since it's bad protocol to snipe at a rector. The chancellor Bismarck (1815–1898) made Harnack's appointment a question of confidence in his government. The government declared that in the universities there must be freedom of scholarship and no obscurantism. Giessen gave Bismarck a doctorate for his courageous stand.

The theological debacle which the conservatives had predicted came four years later. The battle was fought over the Apostles' Creed. A young pastor in Wurttemberg, also a liberal, was fired for denying the virgin birth and for dropping the Apostles' Creed from the liturgy. Students asked Harnack for his comments and some bright fellow published them soon afterwards. Harnack said, "Oh, well, the Apostles' Creed is an affirmation of personal faith and personal values." We hear in this the voice of Ritschl: theological statements are value judgments. The creed begins, "I believe"; therefore, the argument went, it is personal and can't be made mandatory for the whole church. Harnack said that he himself was uneasy with the virgin birth. A word-by-word recitation of the Apostles' Creed, he added, can even go against personal conscience, and that would be the worst sin: to violate one's own convictions. (We need to notice here that, though the idea of sin is present, there has been a subtle change in the definition of conscience; Harnack has shifted from a moral definition of conscience to an intellectual one.) Nevertheless, Harnack told his students not to create a revolution, but to study diligently (again echoing Ritschl), and then stick to their convictions once they become pastors. In this way, they would all see a wonderful future unfolding for the church. The mandate, as Harnack saw it, was to shape the next generation.

In response to the ruckus the Apostles' Creed debate stirred up, the government came up with a Solomonic solution. They couldn't of course remove Harnack, but they added another chair in Berlin and forced a conservative on the liberal faculty. This was the "punishment professor": Adolf Schlatter.

In the winter of 1899–1900, Harnack gave his famous lectures on the "Essence of Christianity." They were a popular summary of Harnack's gospel, and an immediate best-seller (translated into 16 languages and republished 60–70 years later by Bultmann himself).

Yet it is tempting to see these lectures as aluminum compared with the heavy bronze of Ritschl's theology. Harnack's is light-weight theology. He said it is only the Father, and not the Son, who belongs in the gospel.

The Post-Ritschl Liberal School: Weiss and Harnack

We are not to believe in Jesus; we believe like Jesus. His emphases are: "God the Father," providence, sonship (of the Christian), and the infinite worth of the human soul—in such tenets, Harnack said, the whole of the Christian gospel is expressed. (Of course the idea of God's wrath is long gone among all these people.) As in Ritschl, Harnack's emphasis is not on salvation but on providence. His is a non-dogmatic Christianity.

He wanted to do away with all the structure of dead orthodoxy, and instead focus on the ethical exemplariness of Jesus the man. And his sources for truth were both the Bible and humanism. Harnack would quote as easily the famous phrase, "Be noble, helpful and good" from the German poet laureate Goethe as he would the synoptic gospels. That phrase, he said, captured the message of the gospel anyways. So we see here a strong optimism in man. He had no room for the doctrine of sin or even original sin—which he considered gloomy and called "a foolish doctrine." He, therefore, had not much room for atonement, either.

In light of all this, it is not surprising that Harnack became the leading spokesman for the theology of mediation—that is, between Christianity and humanist culture. While Schleiermacher had attempted this, in Harnack it reached its pinnacle. Harnack's theology, and the theology of his immediate colleagues, has been labeled "culture Protestantism."

Harnack, due to his fame and his residing in Berlin, became a counsellor to the emperor and a star of both the court and educated high society. He actually left the teaching of theology and, in 1905, became the General Director of the national libraries. In 1914, Harnack wrote the emperor's speech to the nation on the eve of World War I, the day of mobilization of military forces. He was a signatory to "The Declaration of the Ninety-one"—a declaration signed by prominent intellectuals in support of the Kaiser and the

German cause. He moved even farther into secular culture after World War I, organizing Germany's large-scale scientific research.

Germany has independent research institutions (now called Planck Institutes after Max Planck, who formulated the quantum theory; they were formerly called Kaiser Wilhelm Institutes). People who work there have no teaching obligations. Harnack invented these institutes, and they became instrumental in rebuilding Germany's national honour after the war. Germany was demoralized after World War I, but Harnack laid the groundwork for the country's large-scale research, which has paid cultural dividends for generations to come.

THE ABRUPT DECLINE OF HARNACK'S INFLUENCE

Harnack's theological influence died after World War I. His "large masses" of historical material could not prevent the rise of a "new myth" in theology. The vast destruction on the battlefield of World War I and the deep miseries at home destroyed the general optimistic view of man and the idealism which was the basis of Harnack's theology.

His theology matched the bright years of progress around the turn of the century, but it could not stand the enormous moral destruction and humiliation of World War I. In addition, the revolution of 1918 in Germany deeply shattered the values of the bourgeoisie.

The executioner of liberalism came from the ranks of liberalism itself: Karl Barth. The year 1914 was a major shock to Barth. He had been a student of Harnack's in Berlin, but then the war broke out. How, Barth asked, could God be claimed by the respective sides in the war? Suddenly it dawned on Barth that culture Christianity is not mediation between Christianity and culture, but rather the dissolution of Christianity into culture. Christianity gets swallowed.

The Post-Ritschl Liberal School: Weiss and Harnack

Barth's 1922 edition (the second edition) of his Romans commentary, an existentialist protest against theological liberalism, stressed the antithesis of culture and religion. In 1923, Barth and Harnack waged, through open letters, a public war of words and ideas. Harnack felt that Barth was driving theology back into unscientific irrationalism, creating a new barbarism which was destroying all of theology's scholarly achievement and respectability in society. Harnack wrote *Fifteen Questions to the Despisers of Scientific Theology Among Theologians*. Barth came back with similar vehemence. A mere five years later, it was clear Barth had won; Harnack could not stop the advance of dialectical theology.

Dialectical theology was pessimistic. The hope for a golden age in theology had been flooded out by what Harnack called a new irrationalism. In 1929, he wrote, "I would never have thought that a kind of speculation could again arise among us for which I certainly have no antennae." A generation moved swiftly in the opposite direction from Harnack, who died in 1930. One of his students (from 1924–1925), Dietrich Bonhoeffer, spoke at his graveside.

Harnack represents early twentieth century liberalism. He represents a devout and highly ethical liberalism—he would, for example, have daily family prayer. Such behavior is mostly absent among today's liberals. Yet Harnack's devoutness was often fed as much by culture as by the gospel. And he, and those he represented, were weak doctrinally, coming dangerously close to the precipice of syncretism, to mixing Christianity and the ideas in vogue at the time.

Meditation
Psalm 124:1–3, 8

> If the Lord had not been on our side,
>   let Israel say,
> if the Lord had not been on our side
>   when men attacked us,
> when their anger flared against us,
>   they would have swallowed us alive . . .
> Our help is in the name of the Lord
>   the maker of heaven and earth.

There are things which rise up against us, like adverse conditions, physical weakness, disorientation, bewilderment. At the end of the term, we need a phrase like,

> Our help is in the name of the Lord
>   the maker of heaven and earth.

Things which arise from within us and come out of our own heart are even more perplexing and difficult than the external things. There too,

> Our help is in the name of the Lord
>   the maker of heaven and earth.

He's the one who can overcome those things within ourselves which rise up against us.

Chapter Four

THE EVANGELICAL ALTERNATIVE
*An Overview of Evangelical Theology on the
Continent in the Nineteenth Century*

Throughout this time—the last half of the nineteenth century—there was a third pillar in theology, evangelicalism. The story here has never been told. The relevant books by Cremer and Schlatter have never been translated. So here, we will sketch the story.

By 1850, there was no longer any evangelical representation in the universities. Before the middle of the nineteenth century, there had been evangelical representation in the universities, mostly as a result of the broad influence of August Tholuck (1799–1877), the theologian of the revival. In the years after 1850, Europe was dominated by political and theological reactionism as a result of the abortive political revolution in 1848 and of the advance of Lutheran orthodox confessionalism. It was a time when, as in our own time, evangelicalism turned conservative—but it must be stressed that evangelicalism is not the same thing as conservatism. At any rate, evangelical influence was never established in theology after 1850.

Tholuck was an exegete; he was not a systematician, and it is the systematicians who shape the next generation in the church. He helped form a large body of clergy, but he did not produce a theologian to succeed him. Yet evangelicalism was not entirely without a systematician. There was Julius Muller (1801–1878), Tholuck's contemporary, whom Tholuck himself won to Christ. Muller made a name for himself with his two-volume *Christian Doctrine of Sin* (1838, 1844). But he suffered a stroke at the age of 55 after a prolonged illness, and stopped writing. His influence dropped off sharply. Muller was an abortive hope for a lasting evangelical presence in theology.

JOHANN TOBIAS BECK (1804–1878)

However, in 1870, a new generation of evangelicals came up. At this time biblically committed theology was considered obsolete. The liberals filtered Scripture through reason; the orthodox filtered it through confessional dogma. The one exception was Johann Tobias Beck at Tübingen. He was a solitary figure in the liberal desert and a latecomer in his influence. Only after his death did he prove to be the starting point for a new departure in theology. He was a contemporary of August Tholuck, Julius Muller and, also, of Ludwig Feuerbach (1804–1872), the famous critic of religion.

Johann Tobias Beck came from a simple background socially and, because of illness, was thrown into self-study. So he by-passed most of the theological fashions of the day. He just studied by reading, and his reading was almost exclusively Scripture. He read the Bible so brilliantly, with such depth of insight and strength of memory, that he simply sat for the final exam and passed. Then he turned to the pastoral ministry. In 1836, the Swiss for the first time tried to counter the influence of liberalism and rationalist theology by establishing a privately endowed chair at Basel, an endowment which is allowed by the Swiss constitution but is not possible in Germany. Beck was invited over from his parish work to be the first professor in the chair. He also taught at the new Basel missionary seminary, which sent out missionaries to India and West Africa. So he was right in the heart of evangelical endeavour—though he soon upset other evangelicals by his criticism of missionary busy-ness.

He was invited into the lion's den at Tübingen (his old university) in 1843. A liberal fortress, where Ritschl had gone as a young man, everybody thought that Beck would be broken and down-and-out within a few months. To everyone's surprise, he developed a friendly relationship with the liberal giant himself, Ferdinand Christian Baur. At Tübingen, Beck slowly began to exercise an influence; in time, he had the largest number of students in any classroom. His influence spread: it was strong in Tübingen's province of Wurttemberg, but also reached Switzerland; he even had a hand in the revival in Finland 2000 miles away. He shaped both clergy and a small group of theologians. Cremer, Kahler, Schlatter—all at some point studied under Beck. Beck's method was biblicism—that is, developing a systematic theology entirely from Scripture. It was, in some ways, Biblical Theology. He makes no reference to any theologian or Reformer, but only to Scripture.

There was, in fact, a strong evangelical heritage in Tübingen despite its reigning liberalism. These "biblicists of Wurttemberg" were presaged by Johann Albrecht Bengel, a biblicist whose exegetical commentaries on the whole New Testament are still worth reading. They are a treasure chest of very sharp, terse, precise observations. Beck built on the groundwork of Bengel.

Biblicism meant, in practical terms, independence from the Protestant Reformation. Beck was the first in the history of Protestantism who dared to criticize Luther's doctrine of justification. He said justification in Scripture is not merely declarative, but effective. It changes the person.

It not only declares them right, but makes them righteous. Such an announcement was, among Protestants, terrible: it came close to what Roman Catholics said. Beck was also the first in Protestantism to insist on ethics as a horizon for Old Testament and New Testament theology. The whole of Scripture would be misunderstood, he claimed, if not read within the horizon of ethics: man is evil but he ought to be good. How does man become good? Through full—that is, biblical—justification.

Beck was a solitary figure. He had to be, because he was merciless in his criticism of the times. He railed against evangelical superficiality. Beck had in his mind a dark picture of the coming de-Christianization of Europe. He prophesied, in the face of the contemporary church triumphalism, the seeping secularism that would one day deaden the church. He was a thoroughly independent mind, a Jeremiah.

THE NEW GENERATION: AUGUST HERMANN CREMER (1834–1903)

Cremer was a contemporary of the other influential evangelical theologian, Martin Kähler (1835–1912). But Cremer was the first to accomplish a breakthrough for evangelical theology and make it a publicly visible alternative to Harnack as well as, to some degree, Lutheran orthodox confessionalism.

He was a Westphalian. Westphalia is in the West, part of the North Rhine. Geography shapes character to an extent, and those who come from Westphalia are by nature independent, strong-willed, and persistent to the point of stubbornness. Cremer was also intelligent. He came from an evangelical home; his mother was a Jewish Christian.

His neighbours called his family's house the "pietist's hostel" because there were always missionaries on furlough

The Evangelical Alternative

and itinerant preachers staying there. A house church also met in their home; they studied Scripture, talked—like the Methodists—about progress in personal sanctification, and discussed world events in the light of the advance of God's kingdom and mission. Cremer also went to a Christian school—not normally a possibility on the continent at that time.

After graduating from the Christian school, Cremer studied at Tübingen—along with Beck—and at Halle, under Tholuck. This is where he formed a life-long friendship with Martin Kähler. He was such a brilliant student of evangelical commitment that the head of the German Bible Society financed his doctorate. An evangelical could earn a doctorate, but was rarely admitted to a liberal faculty to teach. Cremer was denied a professorship and so became a rural pastor. He was placed in a liberal congregation which was morally rowdy and spiritually asleep. He had his windows broken after disciplining the worst excesses. He continued with serious preaching and persistent, loyal, spiritual nurturing over a period of years and won the people's hearts. A wave of new spiritual life swept through the congregation. On the basis of these experiences, Cremer—in contrast to Beck—returned to a more Lutheran view of justification, emphasizing the grace of God and forgiveness. But he continued to stress the importance of Christian ethics which he had learned from Beck. He said, "Sermons must address not the mind, but the conscience. And they must awaken repentance and faith." So, though he no longer thought, as Beck did, in terms of effective righteousness, he at least thought in terms of realistic repentance.

Cremer also continued Beck's biblical emphasis. We must, he believed, begin with Scripture, not the Reformational confessions. For this reason, he began his lifetime's famous work, *The Biblico-Theological Lexicon of New Testament Greek*. It began as a small volume with the main concepts of New Testament theology, but in his lifetime went through eleven editions. On the basis of Cremer's book, the government in Berlin appointed him to a professorship in 1870. The authorities, stricken by a sudden attack of fairness, invited him in order to give evangelical theology a chance. But so that not too much damage would be done, they gave him to Germany's tiniest theological faculty, a mere seventeen theological students—at the University of Grieswald in Pomerania (along the Baltic). But even that was too much for the local liberal university senate and the magistrate. They vigorously opposed the appointment. Cremer had to sue for the keys to the vicarage and for his salary. For two years his case was in court.

At one point the Pomeranians themselves, like Westphalians also known for their stubbornness, sent him a message: We'll see who has more stamina. In the end, Cremer did.

His influence grew over the years, and he even succeeded in placing evangelicals in all the chairs of the theological faculty. In order to provide a visible evangelical alternative, he stuck to Grieswald, turning down offers to positions in other universities. Schlatter and others came. During Cremer's time there, Grieswald grew to 300 theological students.

Cremer became influential among his students through three tools: his systematic theology lectures; his homiletics seminars; and his regular Sunday sermons in the university church. He said his aim was to provide a place for the gospel to hibernate. In addition to his *Lexicon*, he wrote *The Pauline Doctrine of Justification*, and published a little monograph (recently republished), *The Attributes of God* (1897). He also did battle against liberalism and wrote *A Reply to Harnack on the Essence of Christianity*. In addition, he was one of the remarkable evangelicals who had a strong concern for social ethics. He took a strong position on the social questions of the day and wrote a little book on the Christian view of property and possessions. He was also very involved in church politics and publicly fought the Minister of Religion and Cults who tried to force pastors to officiate at remarriages of divorcees.

Yet he lamented that evangelicals cared so little for serious theological work, and that for most the only effort to save the church from the plunderings of liberalism was carried out through mere administrative measures. Without solid theology, Cremer saw, politicking would not help.

ADOLF SCHLATTER (1852–1938)

His Life

Adolf Schlatter was born in St. Gall, in eastern Switzerland, the seventh of eight children. He grew up in a family of committed Christians. His grandmother corresponded with some of the leading theologians of her day. His parents, however, were members of different denominations. Adolf's father had been re-baptized—a terrible thing in a Reformed country—and had become a lay preacher in a small free church. His mother and the children continued in the Reformed national church, which practised infant baptism. Schlatter later said that this taught him an early lesson: Christianity is more than any one particular denomination. And Christianity doesn't fail when one denomination goes down.

His father was a pharmacist who took his children on nature walks—a rare thing at the time—and instilled in his children a deep love for God's creation. Adolf Schlatter was a gifted student but found school terribly boring, with one exception: a young Greek teacher who privately read the Greek New Testament with him outside school. This teacher himself later became a famous professor of comparative languages. Schlatter intended to follow this teacher and also study comparative languages, not theology.

There was, he saw, a danger of losing your faith in the study of theology. But one of Schlatter's sisters challenged him on this, and so he decided to try theology. He said this decision to trust was his conversion experience.

Schlatter went to Basel first, and then to Tübingen where he studied with Beck. After the normal academic Triennium, the three years of theological studies (students then learned Latin, Greek and Hebrew in high school), Schlatter took a position as an assistant pastor in Zürich in a Reformed church. His boss was a committed liberal, and he was faced with a problem which exists in many denominations today: how to get along with someone from the other school of thought. Schlatter's resolve was, "Do not break unity but clearly demonstrate the differences in faith." So, instead of splitting off as he might have done had he lived in North America, he stayed in the same denomination. After this, he pastored a small church in a village near Lake Constance for three years. Then he was called to the University of Berne, the capital of Switzerland (in the same way that Beck had been called to Basel).

In Berne, Schlatter discovered a group of strategically thinking evangelicals. None were prominent theologians. They founded a Christian high school, a teachers' training college, and endowed a chair in the faculty of theology to counter the overwhelming influence of liberalism. They wanted to safeguard the next generation in the school and in the church. Schlatter needed a doctorate in order to take up the position, so he wrote his doctoral thesis in three months. It was republished in 1888 with the title *John the Baptist* and reprinted after 1945. The Swiss authorities had a very strong sense of justice and were bound by existing laws, and admitted an evangelical to the faculty. When he presented himself, the Minister of Education said he would never be made a professor because he knew the pietists were praying for that. Schlatter knew he was at the periphery of the theological arena.

He took to writing as well as teaching. "Even if I have no lectern," he said, "I have a pen." His first book was *Faith in the New Testament*, which was the basis of many of his later corrections of traditional Protestant theology. At the same time, he began to transcribe the popular expositions of the New Testament which he gave week by week in a house Bible study group. This became *The Popular Exposition of the New Testament* (13 volumes, German). He wrote by hand all his sermons and commentaries, dictating nothing.

He went on to Grieswald in 1888 to support Cremer; five years later he went on to Berlin as the conservative "punishment" professor.

As Beck had befriended Baur, contrary to all expectations, so too Schlatter came into close personal contact with Harnack. The liberals generally despised Schlatter (*Faith in the New Testament* was butchered in the liberal review), but Harnack knew a good historian when he saw one and invited Schlatter, to the astonishment of the entire liberal establishment, to publish in his series. In addition to his work in New Testament, Schlatter taught and wrote in the fields of dogmatics and ethics. He wrote four volumes during those years in Berlin; all have been recently reprinted. He also published a famous monograph series, *Beitrage zur Förderung Christlicher Theologie* (*Contributions to the Furtherance of Christian Theology*). Throughout that time, he had strong contacts with the general evangelical movement, mission societies, and the young YMCA. Then, in 1898, he was called to Tübingen. This was also a new chair to counter liberalism, established by the king of Württemberg, and was given a cold reception by the intellectual establishment there. As with Beck, it took a long time for him to establish his influence, but eventually it grew out of bounds. He often had 800 students in his lecture hall, and shaped a whole generation of evangelical pastors.

He remained at Tübingen until his retirement in 1922. During this time he published *The Church in the New Testament Period*. Then he delved into the history of philosophy to see how far modern philosophy could be utilized by Christians. His book stemming from this is called *The Philosophical Work Since Descartes: Its Moral and Religious Results*. Along with these, he also published several books of sermons.

There was an exceptional harvest which Schlatter reaped in his old age. At 75, he accepted an invitation to help with a girls' group. So at age 75, with his long beard and grandfatherly appearance, he began youth work. At the same time, he was very involved with a house church. He continued to teach from age 70 to 78, and, in his last eight years (age 78 to 86), he penned his most famous magisterial series of Greek exegetical commentaries. In 1929 he published *Matthew*, an absolutely foundational commentary. In 1930, *John*. One year later, *Luke*. In 1932, a commentary on James. In 1933 (the national revolution) he didn't publish. In 1934, he published another big commentary, on Corinthians. Because he was sorry that nothing had been published in 1933, he published two in 1935, one on Mark and another essential, and large, commentary on Romans. In 1936, he wrote on Timothy and Titus, and in 1937, 1 Peter. Three of them (Matthew, Romans, and Corinthians) are of especially lasting value.

Adolf Schlatter impressed his contemporaries as a man of utter seriousness and at the same time of remarkable joyfulness in faith.

He was also, like Beck before him, known for his independent positions in scholarship and church. Schlatter was the closest thing to an evangelical theologian on the continent in the early twentieth century. He was a towering exegete and a powerful and seminal systematician.

Schlatter's Theology

Schlatter was world famous as a New Testament scholar. He was the first in the theology of the twentieth century to turn to the early Jewish background to the New Testament, and brought into play here his incredible knowledge of Philo and Josephus, preparing his own concordances on their works. Here, Schlatter was way out in the lead: only in the last few decades has New Testament theology moved away from its preoccupation with the Greek mystery religions and become interested in the thought structures of early Judaism. Schlatter was also one of those rare people who knew the whole Greek New Testament by heart; his own mind was a Greek concordance. On top of all that, he was also a first-class systematician—a little known fact.

Major Concerns in His Theology

Schlatter's first concern was theology. Like Albrecht Ritschl, Schlatter had an awareness of the utter need for theology. And this was no aloof insight, but reflected his wrestling with his evangelical brethren who usually thought otherwise. "Everyone has a theology," he said, even if it is unconscious or shoddy. The task of theology is the clarification of the fundamentals of faith. That task involves the constant re-examination of our convictions in the light of the New Testament.

Schlatter wanted to establish the utmost importance of theology in the activities of the church. Because theology clarifies and purifies our convictions, it must, in the life of the church, come before social reform, liturgical reform, or church politics. Theology, that is, teaching, comes first. Schlatter, for example, told his evangelical friends who were solely concerned with evangelism and conversion (as are many evangelicals in North America) that we cannot call anyone to conversion unless we are able to say what they are converting to.

Evangelists must at least be able to answer the questions, "What does it mean to be a Christian?" and "How shall we then live?" Schlatter battled against decisionism, where people are urged to make a decision, though often they are not clear what they are deciding for or against. This is just another form of subjectivism. (Actually, decisionism is very close to the Bultmann school's brand of faith.)

Schlatter thought evangelicals needed teaching and deepening in their faith. Among other things, this meant that they needed university representation. Not only did the evangelicals need it, but the university also needed it: the word of God was increasingly absent in the universities. Here Schlatter applied the lesson he learned in his first pastorate: fight the fight, not through separation, but within existing structures; this is best done through honest discussion of differences, while being careful to keep the peace.

Theological Method

Schlatter held that the best method for theological understanding is, simply, keen perception. A theologian must be able to see.

Schlatter once mockingly said, "The eye of the wise sees what is there, but the mind of the conceited produces hypotheses." He believed that theological cognition only came about through a quiet and sustained observation of the facts. That, of course, meant the facts of Scripture, Scripture being the primary object of perception.

He pursued this principle in radical fashion, even to the extent of eradicating footnotes (which normally discuss the hypotheses of colleagues). The study of the New Testament, he asserted, is not the study of hypotheses about the New

The Evangelical Alternative

Testament. Because Schlatter did not discuss his colleagues' theories and theologies, they despised him.

The process of knowing involves three things: (1) perception; (2) the formation of concepts; and (3) practical application. Practical application is part of the process of cognition. Application gives feedback about whether the concepts formed from observation are correct. Theory has to correspond to reality. Schlatter's position, therefore, has been called "biblical realism." It is a conscious departure from the predominant Kantianism in theology. For the rest of theology, Kantianism had become the starting point for theories of cognition. Schlatter was, therefore, a fairly solitary figure, working with a consciously different epistemology.

Objects of Perception

According to Schlatter, theology's objects of perception are, first, nature, and second, the history of Jesus. Surprisingly, Schlatter begins by saying that nature is an object of theological study. This is contrary to the army of Kantian theologians of his day. Schlatter believed that we can derive knowledge of God from nature; he is one of the rare theologians after Kant to hold to natural theology. Schlatter saw the glory of God revealed in creation more than he saw the fallenness of creation. On this score, he took part in a famous debate when he was over 80.

Karl Heim, one of his close colleagues at the same university, emphasized, on the basis of Romans 8, the groaning of creation: we live in a fallen creation waiting for its salvation. Schlatter, in rebuttal, published an article. "Have you ever," he asked, "heard a cabbage groaning?" He emphasized, in contrast to Heim, the beauty and glory to be seen in creation; this was primary, and reveals the hand of God.

This commitment to nature also, as Schlatter saw it, produced another commitment, the obligation to one's nation. Schlatter emphasized the necessity of participating in the life of the nation, because the nation is our natural habitat and context. "It is not," he said, "outside of God's will that Christians live in their respective nations." He lived this philosophy, too: although born Swiss, he became a German citizen when he took a German university post, in order to be a part of the society in which he was living and teaching. Soon after this, the decision cost him the life of his brilliant eldest son. He was going to be a theologian but was mortally wounded in the first days of World War I. However, Schlatter's patriotism was no blind nationalism. When many around him—including many churchmen and theologians—were getting caught up in the nationalist wave of 1933, the "national revolution" in Germany, he held back. Schlatter was too shrewd to be taken in by the propaganda of 1933. He saw the growing anti-Semitism of the movement, and took a public stand in 1934 against what was happening. Despite his commitment to the nation, or perhaps because of it, he never fell into the nationalist trap.

The second object for theological study, according to Schlatter, is the history of Jesus. The fundament, and indeed the identity, of our faith comes through knowing Jesus. Nature points to God and reminds us of God, but Jesus identifies God for us.

This is the recovery of a classical formula in theology, that nature points to someone. But who that someone is can be identified only through Jesus. Of course, to study the history of Jesus means turning to Scripture. Before all dogma, we first must study Scripture. It is a mistake to immediately mix up Scripture with existing traditions. Scripture should not be read through the glasses of any particular denominational or confessional writings: it must rather be heard by itself. This has been called Schlatter's biblicism.

Objectivism

We still need to look at Schlatter's relationship to evangelicalism. There is in him, first, obvious affinities with evangelicalism. Particularly, his biblicist stance—insisting we listen to the text instead of interpretations of it—is a position close to evangelicalism. But there are also important differences. The first is Schlatter's objectivism. When he claims that nature and the history of Jesus are the prime objects of theology, he is excluding the believer's experience as the prime object. Here he parts company with evangelicals. He comes, rather, with his lack of emphasis on the subjective, very close to orthodoxy and, also, close to Karl Barth. Schlatter's anti-subjectivism became obvious when he went to Grieswald, the German university where Hermann Cremer was building the evangelical alternative. Schlatter showed little appreciation for the necessity of personal confession of sins. At that time, Lutheran orthodoxy insisted on individual confession of sins before receiving the Lord's Supper. Schlatter disturbed his friend Cremer by coming to the altar without having been in the manse the evening before for personal confession of sins. In some ways, he was more objectivist than even the conservative Lutherans.

His objectivism, though, went beyond a refusal to make individual confession of sins. In fact, Schlatter shifted the whole structure of theology away from Reformational theology. His theology does not, as does Reformation theology, revolve around the axis of sin and justification. The doctrine of justification has been called the *articulus stantis et cadentis ecclesiae*, the article by which the church stands or falls. That was of course Protestantism's distinguishing doctrine in Reformation times. But Schlatter moved away from this. Similar to Karl Barth, Schlatter's theology is not structured around sin and grace. Soteriology is no longer central. In its place, Schlatter placed the "knowledge of Jesus." What matters is to know Jesus. Schlatter's objectivism also came out clearly when his prospective employers at Bern (that responsible group who had set up a chair of theology) first asked him to give witness to his faith. Their question: "What do you believe?" He answered in a way which he later said was both necessary and typical. He spoke of a personal relationship to Christ, but he formulated it with a historic text—the second article of Luther's Smaller Catechism:

> I believe that Jesus Christ, true God, begotten of the Father from eternity and also true man, born of the virgin Mary, is my Lord, who has redeemed me, a lost and condemned creature, delivered me and freed me from all sins, from death, and from the power of the devil, not with silver and gold, but with his holy and precious blood and with his innocent sufferings and death, in order that I may be his, live under him in his kingdom, and serve him in everlasting righteousness, innocence and blessedness, even as he has risen from the dead and lives and reigns to all eternity. This is most certainly true.

He simply recited this. It was a personal statement, but it was clothed in the garment of an objective statement of faith. Schlatter felt that was the limit to which anyone could allow personal experience to speak in theology. The "I" was there, but it was bounded in by the confession of the church.

Schlatter and Scripture

Schlatter's second divergence from evangelicalism was his attitude toward Scripture. He claimed his use of Scripture was different from the pietists and the evangelicals. He said he stood between the liberal's critique of Scripture and the pietists' legalistic use of it. His approach, instead, was unprejudiced perception.

Perception, for instance, made him recognize multiple sources in the Pentateuch: this was unheard of for an evangelical. Schlatter was criticized by the liberals as being a biblicist and by conservative evangelicals as being a criticist. He felt evangelicals were pressing Scripture into a harmonizing doctrinal scheme and were as a result losing Scripture's richness. Schlatter said he saw behind this a certain honourable timidity on the part of evangelicals. For fear of losing biblical substance, they retained the form—particularly, for instance, the old Lutheran translation. But Schlatter's greatest criticism of conservative evangelicals was that they left out the Holy Spirit who interprets Scripture for today's situation. Evangelicals and orthodox alike did that. There was a fear in the church, maybe an honourable fear, but a fear nonetheless, of the Holy Spirit. Schlatter felt that the liberals censored Scripture and the evangelicals only repeated it—which was legalism. Schlatter, in contrast, said Scripture shows us the Son of God who did not have the law of God above him, but the effectiveness of God within him. And the Holy Spirit re-presents Scripture for us today. So Schlatter deplored the traditionalist and orthodox element in evangelicalism which always comes to the fore when evangelicalism engages in the struggle with liberalism.

A Critique of Lutheran Reformational Orthodoxy

Schlatter, picking up on the doubts which his teacher at Tübingen, Johann Tobias Beck, had expressed, was uneasy about the Reformational orthodoxy's declarative or forensic understanding of justification. He blamed a mere declarative understanding of justification for the weakness of ethics in Protestantism.

Protestantism's great emphasis on justification diminishes the importance of regeneration. A sole emphasis on faith swallows up love. There is, Schlatter said, no room for love of God in Protestantism. When faith alone is stressed, man's reason is addressed but not his will. Both the orthodox and the liberal inherited the ancient Greek primacy of reason over will, which leads to a neglect of ethics. But this neglect of ethics, Schlatter said, is not the signature of Scripture. The church sees little of the new life of discipleship because they teach it little, or not at all. Schlatter, as an example, mentioned the traditional Lutheran interpretation of the Sermon on the Mount, which was one-sidedly accusatory. The Reformers treated the Sermon on the Mount not as a call to new life, but as an exposure of human sin.

In addition to all Schlatter's work in the New Testament, he single-handedly launched a biblical criticism of the Reformation. If theology's task is to be always examining our existing convictions in the light of the New Testament, then nothing can be spared: we must be willing even to criticize the roots of Protestantism.

Schlatter's first step in this criticism was his publication in 1899 of *The Christian's Service in the Older Dogmatics* (that is, Reformational orthodoxy of the 17th century). This is a critique of Reformational orthodoxy. He observes a dry intellectualism in its theology: thinking is stronger than acting. If there is any ethic, it is an ethic of avoidance, a negative ethic, a list of what we must not do. Ethics is reduced to the commandments and is therefore very legalistic. There's no conception of the living will of God, of the guidance of the Holy Spirit. And, as an outfall of that, there is no vision for missions in the ethics of Reformational orthodoxy. As well, the lack of the doctrine of the Holy Spirit means that they must replace the teaching of the Holy Spirit by the doctrine of ministry. The ordained minister takes the place of the Holy Spirit. The church, then, is reduced to a

The Evangelical Alternative

one-man show. Schlatter was the first to criticize the one-man principle in Protestantism.

Schlatter's second step in his critique was his publication of a little monograph on Luther's interpretation of Romans (1515–1516). Luther's commentary had just been rediscovered and was published shortly before World War I. Schlatter, instead of celebrating the 400th anniversary of the Reformation in 1917, strongly criticized it, and Luther's interpretation of Romans in particular.

He pointed out the lack in Luther's interpretation of the biblical relationship between justification and sanctification. Schlatter had already seen this lack of a link between justification and regeneration in Reformational orthodoxy; now he discovered that the lack began in Luther himself. What Schlatter first thought was a defect of the pupils, he now saw in the master.

A third step in Schlatter's criticism is his 1935 commentary on Romans; this is a running critique of Martin Luther. Schlatter was one of the very rare evangelical theologians who stood independent of the Protestant tradition. Our love for Luther, he said, cannot be allowed to limit the church.

Schlatter died in 1938. His death meant the abrupt end of the evangelical alternative. Two of his closest colleagues died about the same time. The younger pastors whom Schlatter influenced were drawn into the confessing church and from there into Barthianism in the 1930s.

Nothing in evangelical theology equals the comprehensiveness of Schlatter's work. But, because of his theological nonconformism, he was not heeded during his lifetime. Only now is his influence on New Testament scholarship beginning to be felt; it has influenced even liberal theologians such as Käsemann and especially the present giant in New Testament at Tübingen, Peter Stuhlmacher. Yet Schlatter the systematician is still awaiting rediscovery.

The Situation of Evangelical Theology After Schlatter

Schlatter's death brought a breakdown in evangelical theology on the same scale as the breakdown in liberal theology in the 1920s (when Harnack's theology lost its grip). In the German-speaking world today there are, with the possible exception of Peter Beyerhaus, no evangelicals in posts of theological faculties.

Beyerhaus is an orthodox Conservative Lutheran who has turned semi-evangelical. And his chair is in Missions and Ecumenism, which is on the theological periphery, a sort of a fifth wheel in Protestant theology. As well, there are practically no evangelical facilities outside the universities, only two or three little seminaries for some of the free churches. These are notoriously small and do not contribute to the general discussion. What is worse, not only are there no evangelicals in the faculties, but there are very few who would be eligible for university teaching. The situation is similar to when Harnack was called to Berlin. The conservatives had nothing to offer in his place. Today evangelicals, which make up the vast mass of foot soldiers of the Protestant church, are no longer accustomed to doing theology. Every year there are hundreds of young men and women convinced through evangelical preaching and evangelical youth work to go into ministry; they attend universities and end up deformed by the Bultmannian school.

Schlatter, when asked why he had no successor, said he dared call no one away from parish work to the university. Perhaps he forgot that he owed his own life's work to some evangelicals who dared call him away from his parish work into the chair at Berne.

What influence has Schlatter had in North America? Very little of Schlatter's work, either in New Testament exegesis or in theology, has had any impact in North America. Yet Schlatter would be a first-class resource in meeting the challenges of liberal theology. Schlatter himself said that we need theology both for the training of the evangelist himself and for rooting the faith of the evangelized. The need for both—training up and rooting down—increases with the advance of secularism. John Wesley said, "Evangelism without teaching [that is, theology] means begetting children for the evil one." Schlatter would help greatly in the teaching.

KARL HEIM (1874–1958)

Karl Heim belongs to this evangelical alternative, though almost a generation after Schlatter. Schlatter died in 1938 and Heim retired in 1939. Then the war came. After that, theological groups in the church were completely rearranged. The Barthians were in positions of church government. Although Heim wrote after the war, he no longer had much effect on the church. So Schlatter's death was really the end of the evangelical school of theology.

Heim's Biography

Karl Heim was born of a family of evangelical clergy. He himself, just after he graduated from high school, was converted to an actively evangelical Christianity under the preaching of a famous evangelist at a student conference in 1893. He studied theology at Tübingen, then became one of the first traveling secretaries for the German equivalent of InterVarsity, which had just been founded. He came into contact with scientists at the graduate level. In 1903, after four years of travelling, he was made the inspector of a student residence at Halle, the old seedbed of evangelicalism. He used his time to write his second thesis, which qualified him to teach theology. In 1907, he became an assistant professor, and in 1904, he had already published his first book, *The World View of the Future*, which received considerable attention. He gave his impressions of all those discussions with the young scientists. But typical of the fate of an evangelical, he wasn't made a full professor until age 40, at Münster. In 1920, he joined Adolf Schlatter at Tübingen and taught there another nineteen years. He continued his work for InterVarsity, and especially for the International Council of Missions. As such, he participated as a delegate in the Jerusalem missionary council of 1928. Many of his books have been translated in English as a result of a lecture tour he gave in the United States in 1935. This tour was so successful that he was invited to take up a professorship at Princeton, but he declined this. He died in 1958.

Heim's Theological Concerns

Heim's first concern was evangelism on the level of philosophy and science. In some ways he is one of the few apologists in modern Protestant theology. His books make frequent reference to Kant, Kierkegaard, and other philosophers. His aim is to make atheistic thought insecure, to lead in strict logical reasoning to a point where a person must either despair of making sense of the world or come to faith in Jesus Christ. His concern was to make secular philosophy uncertain, to make room for faith within a modern scientific world view. His books show an enormously broad encounter with modern science. He was said to be the only theologian to have understood Einstein. In pursuit of this attempt to make room for faith within a modern scientific world view, he not only came up with arguments, he also developed a new concept of the dimensions of reality which would leave room for faith. There were three levels: (1) the world of objects, (2) human relationships (Buber's I-Thou plays an important role here), and (3) the level of the things of God. In terms of this endeavour, the magnum opus is *Evangelical Faith and Contemporary Thought* (six volumes), written over a span of twenty years (1931–1952). He began it

The Evangelical Alternative

at age 57. Heim was also one of the very few who picked up on the battle against secularism at an early stage. He made, in a 1928 lecture delivered at the Jerusalem conference, a plea for Christians to recognize the upcoming tide of secularism. Even then he was aware of the phenomenon that secularism always comes in two phases: first intoxication, and then meaninglessness. So his first concern was with gospel and culture.

Heim's actual dogmatics emphasize both the reality of the satanic in the world and the victory of Christ. Christ, he said, publicly assumed power over the forces of this world. Heim understands Jesus' triumph to be over not just sin, but evil. At Calvary, Christ took away our guiltiness, but he also crushed the devil. This is, of course, a critique of the Protestant Reformers' narrow understanding of soteriology as mere justification. Heim, in contrast to that, recovers "classic" Christology, a term used by the Swedish Lutheran theologian Gustaf Aulen. Aulén said there are different types of Christology. The "classic" type, the christology of the early fathers, described Jesus not as victim but as victor. In *Christus Victor* (1931), Aulén describes Jesus' victory over sin, the world, and the devil. Christ's work is not just shrunken to justification of the guilty. Karl Heim shared Aulén's view.

Heim also published a series of sermons and had a great deal of success and resonance among the student body. He had vast audiences and did a lot of student counseling. Together with Schlatter he formed a whole generation of evangelical pastors. But like Schlatter, Heim had no real successor in the university. He was followed by Kaberle at Tübingen, whose story is one of the defeat of an evangelical theology. The years after the war at Tübingen were years of struggle between the remaining conservative professors and the up-and-coming Bultmannians. The Bultmannians in their heyday had no respect for human blood. They publicly jeered and mocked the conservative professors and made disparaging remarks about their theological ability. There was tremendous infighting.

One New Testament professor, sneering, said, "Oh yes, you should hear my colleague Kaberle playing cello!"—the implication being that there was nothing to be gained from hearing him lecture; his only excellence was playing cello. Kaberle actually was a musical person (his son is a prominent musician in Germany today) and with this sensitive nature couldn't stand the atmosphere at Tübingen. He left before retirement. Otto Michel (author of commentaries on Romans and Hebrews) stayed and fought, although he found it very difficult. If Kaberle had been able to hang in one more year, Michel would have had a chance to influence the selection of Kaberle's successor (because as dean the following year he would have had two votes). But Kaberle bailed out. And that meant the end of the story of Schlatter and Heim and their dominance up until 1938. There is now a small Karl Heim Society in Germany where evangelical scientists and theologians meet, but it is outside of the university. It is more like an esoteric Karl Heim fan club. Evangelicals, in the wake of men like Heim and Kaberle, became a vast mass of foot soldiers without general staff.

Meditation
Psalms 128:1–2 & 127:1–2

Blessed are all who fear the Lord,
    who walk in his ways.
You will eat the fruit of your labour;
    blessings and prosperity will be yours (Ps. 128:1–2)

Unless the Lord builds the house,
    its builders labour in vain.
Unless the Lord watches over the city,
    the watchmen stand guard in vain.
In vain you rise early
    and stay up late,
toiling for food to eat
    for he grants sleep to those he loves (Ps. 127:1–2)

These two psalms seem to form a dialectic which is most appropriate in these days. Ps. 128:1–2 has the strongest possible encouragement to diligence. You will eat the fruit of your labour when it comes time. "Blessed are all who fear the Lord." It is the strongest encouragement to diligence. "In vain you rise early." It is diligence, and for the rest, you just put it into the hand of the Lord. Don't think that your own diligence will save you. In the last analysis, you need to have a distance between yourself and your struggle and your achievement, a distance between yourself and your work. It is a marvelous thing in Christianity that a person is not identified by his or her work.

Chapter Five

KARL BARTH (1886–1968)

Karl Barth was born May 10, 1886, and died on December 9 or 10—sometime in the night and in his sleep—in 1968. The son of an evangelical professor of New Testament, Fritz Barth, Karl was born in Basel and grew up in Berne. As happens so often, the conservative son turned liberal when studying theology (the same, as we have seen, was true of Ritschl and Harnack).

Karl Barth first studied at Berne. But he wanted to get a taste of the great wide world and went to Berlin, the most renowned faculty at that time. He immediately became Harnack's pupil. His father was not pleased, and so his father had him commandeered to Schlatter at Tübingen for the next term, to erase liberalism's impressions on him. But Karl returned after the summer term, unchanged and defiant. So his father gave up the struggle and allowed him to go to Marburg, the centre of liberal theology, and at the time a hothouse of philosophical and theological Kantianism. Famous philosophers like Hermann Cohen (1842–1918) and Paul Natorp (1854–1924) were there. Wilhelm Hermann (the student of Tholuck and then Ritschl) was Barth's teacher (in the narrow sense, serving as the link between Ritschl and Barth). Hermann combined liberalism and a more experiential theology as an inheritance from pietism.

Barth, after completing his studies, showed he was right in the heart of liberalism: he became assistant editor to Martin Rader (another professor at Marburg) for the magazine *The Christian World*, the leading magazine of liberal churchmanship. Barth himself published a major essay in it while still a student. (It was published in two installments. Barth always wrote lengthy texts. He couldn't put pen to paper without writing fifty pages.) The article includes a paean to liberal theology. Our church fathers, Barth claimed, are now Kant and Schleiermacher.

In 1909, Barth found himself for two years in Calvin's pulpit in Geneva. His preaching was solidly liberal. He married Nelly Hoffmann in Geneva, in 1913. She was only twenty. Then he became a pastor at the industrial village of Safenwil, staying in that pastorate for ten years. Barth was one of those rare breed of professors of theology who have actually worked in the pastorate instead of moving straight from university into academia.

In 1921, he was made professor of Reformed theology (a chair endowed by American donors) at Göttingen, on the basis of the first edition (the really important one) of *Romans* (not the world famous second edition). The notorious second edition in 1922 made him famous. In 1923–1933, with the other heads of the dialectical school of theology, he produced the successful magazine *Zwischen den Zeiten* (*Between the Times*). Bultmann, Brunner, and Barth worked together in that period. In 1925, Barth was made professor of New Testament at Münster in Westphalia, and rapidly became successful as a theological teacher. Five years later, in 1930, he moved to Bonn, and often had about three hundred students in his class. In 1932, the first volume of his *Church Dogmatics* came out.

Karl Barth (1886–1968)

In 1933 the National Socialists took power in Germany. That event was the occasion of Barth's monograph *Theological Existence Today!*, with which he became the backbone of the Christian resistance to the National Socialists' revolution. Two years later, his relationship with the authorities had deteriorated so badly that he was asked to leave his position at the university. Still in possession of his Swiss citizenship, he was able to return to Switzerland.

He was immediately offered a position in Basel, his birthplace. From 1935–1962—twenty-seven years in all—he was a Professor of Theology at Basel. He then had another six years of retirement.

THE PRESUPPOSITIONS

First Presupposition: Liberal Anthropocentrism

In Barth's early years, there were two basic presuppositions underlying his theology. The first was liberal anthropocentrism, a stance which places man at the centre of all things. This was Barth's starting point, the established rule of liberalism at the turn of the century, the main support pillar of culture Protestantism as seen in Harnack. This fact is important: it forms the background to Barth's development. In his article in *The Christian World* at the close of his theological studies, Barth said we have to stand for religious individualism (that is, you must know yourself what religion means to you; no creed can tell you) and for historical relativism (that is, we must apply the whole arsenal of historical tools to the New Testament; we cannot behave as if we were contemporaneous with it). Barth felt he represented the autumn of the age of Schleiermacher. Perhaps his timing was a bit off. Schleiermacher is back in power again today. Rather than the autumn, perhaps it was only an intermezzo in the reign of Schleiermacher.

During Barth's ten years in the country parish, he also strongly participated in the debates among pastors and the provincial synod on the future of the church. That time was also the heyday of his lifelong friendship with Eduard Thurneysen.

Barth and Thurneysen (1888–1975) had met as students at Marburg. While Barth was at Safenwil, Thurneysen was a pastor at a neighbouring village. Every week they would walk several hours to visit with each other, discuss the latest theological developments, and argue together. They would meet half way in the forest. And they wrote to each other. A real correspondence was possible because they had overnight mail delivery. This correspondence makes for good reading, because Barth is unguarded, saying everything he wants to say.

Barth ventured out into the vast field of Germany's theology, while in 1927 Thurneysen was called as pastor to the cathedral in Basel. In the early years, Thurneysen was in many ways Karl Barth's inspiration. Barth was the steamroller—he would see an idea through to its systematic expression. But often the inspiration, and a number of seminal ideas, came from Thurneysen.

Second Presupposition: Religious Socialism

Thurneysen also introduced Karl Barth to religious socialism, the second presupposition underlying Barth's early thinking. At that time religious socialism was not really a school, being only in formation in the 1920s. There were four people who were critical of its development: the two Blumhardts, Johann and Christoph, father and son; Hermann Kutter; and Leonard Ragaz.

Johann Christoph Blumhardt (1805–1880) was a remarkable pastor in Württemberg in the Black Forest. Like Johann Tobias Beck at the University of Tübingen, he was something of a solitary figure in the landscape of the nineteenth century. He was far too original to be counted with the school of evangelical pietism. He was his own man. Beginning as a liberal in his pastorate, he experienced a complete change of view. From then onwards he was the very solitary representative of a realism concerning the kingdom of God.

The phrase "Jesus is Victor," which was later picked up by Karl Barth, and later still was used by Donald Bloesch for the title of one of his books, originated with Blumhardt. There's an interesting story behind it. A young woman in his parish, Gottliebin Dittus, was clearly demon-possessed. She would shout and scream whenever the name of Jesus was mentioned. According to theological liberalism, such things are not supposed to happen: there are no such things as demons. Blumhardt was perplexed and intrigued. Why should she shout at the mention of that name? For a couple of years he ignored the situation. If I don't believe it, he thought, it will go away; it is not real. But it didn't go away. There was a struggle over a period of two years. One time, when he was visiting the house, the girl underwent another beastly attack by the demons. Impatient, he shouted, "Jesus is victor," and immediately she was delivered. She became healthy and, later, when he had his own retreat centre, to which people came from all over, she worked there with him. Blumhardt's personal experience of exorcism created this conviction of the realism of the kingdom of God. Blumhardt began to emphasize theocentric thinking, emphasizing the power of God. And this was important for Barth's later thinking. That Blumhardt also emphasized the power of the work of the Holy Spirit was quite exceptional for the German-speaking theological scene with its Lutheran and Calvinist inheritance.

Christoph Blumhardt (1842–1919) helped his father as a young pastor at this retreat centre at Bad Boll. With his view of the realism of the work of God in history, he was the first German conservative to consider religious socialism. It was the first attempt to re-associate the church with the mass of socialist workers who had been lost by the church. In 1899, he even became a member of the socialist party and a member of the Reichstag from 1900–1906. This was one of the earliest attempts to combine Christianity and socialism. It was not so much philosophical as a concrete, practical alliance with the workers' movement. But Blumhardt later left the socialist party because he felt there was too much atheistic influence (which is clearly the case in the Social Democratic parties on the continent). He felt that, in the last analysis, no cooperation was possible. Socialists generally, because of their different view of God—or disbelief in God—had a different view of man and a different view of society.

In the next generation, Hermann Kutter (1869–1931) was a pupil of the Blumhardts. He was a pastor (and professor for a time) at Zürich, and a famous preacher. He was also influential because of his writing, establishing a whole school of religious socialism with his book *They Must* (that is, they, the socialist workers, must be involved in socialist work, though not in rebellious fashion, but because God is behind the workers' movement of history).

Kutter, when his influence on Barth and Thurneysen was greatest (in the 1920s), was moving away from immediate political questions and issues. His famous phrase was: "God is the social question." He pulled back from political questions, and instead asked another question: "How can we announce God to this generation?" He felt the theological question was more important than any social questions. That emerges again in Karl Barth.

The fourth man, Kutter's immediate colleague, is Leonard Ragaz (1868–1945). If Kutter was the theologian of the religious socialist movement, then Ragaz was the activist. Ragaz, in contrast to Kutter, moved strongly in the other direction, giving up his professorship at Zürich in order to do social work. He also became a famous leader of the pacifist movement of the 1930s. His pragmatism is seen in his collaboration with Lenin when he was in exile in Zürich. It is said that Ragaz is the figure who inspired Lenin to coin the famous phrase "useful idiot" to describe those people who, with ideological reservations, lent their services to his cause.

Karl Barth joined this group with Kutter and Ragaz and lectured to the village and provincial workers' associations. In 1915 he joined the Swiss Socialist Party, which was fairly radical (not far from Marxist-Leninism). He wrote several articles in the workers' newspapers. After the war, in 1918, he helped to organize the local trade union (he was in the middle of the textile industry with powerful industrialists). He even organized a local strike.

BARTH'S RETURN TO THEOLOGY

In 1914, Barth began to return to theology—theology both as a topic and theology with an emphasis on theocentrism. This new departure was triggered by three disappointments in 1914 and later years.

Disappointment With His Teachers

The first disappointment Barth had was with his liberal theological teachers. He was shocked by their attitude at the beginning of World War I. His beloved teacher Harnack wrote the Kaiser's speech on the eve of mobilization and was a signatory to the famous *Manifesto of the Ninety-three* (that is, ninety-three academics pledging loyalty to the national cause). Barth asked himself how God could be employed in the national cause.

Disappointment With International Socialism

At the same time, he was disappointed with international socialism. Before the war, from about 1890, there had been lots of pledges of internationalism in the workers' movement. "We'll never again allow a war of workers against workers." That broke down in the moment of testing. The Social Democrats, contrary to all promises, voted for work credits in the Berlin parliament rather than calling for a general strike as they had promised. In France the same thing happened because Jean Jaurüs, the famous internationalist and leader of the French socialists, was murdered in the first days of the war by an ardent patriot. When the crunch comes, even the most committed social movement may fall before the pressures of indigenous nationalism.

Disappointment With the Church

Thirdly, Barth was disappointed a year or two later with the "insincerity" of the church. In 1916 he complained that everything in the church was a compromise. We needed to take God seriously again. Kutter's emphasis on theology, his inheritance from Blumhardt, was coming to the surface. In his heart Barth had already abandoned liberalism. He discovered that all the other problems of the day need to be replaced by the radical and utterly serious problem of faith. Are we going to live with God, or without him, as has been the case up until now? Let God be God.

That is a task compared with which all the cultural, social and patriotic tasks are child's play. He continued to help the workers, but he had himself arrived at a position where he regarded such help as needed but secondary. In 1918, Barth wrote to Thurneysen, "Oh had we only been reconverted to Scripture earlier so that we would now have a solid bottom under our feet." He went back to reading theology and Scripture. Under those circumstances, he began to write his

Karl Barth (1886–1968)

first book, the first edition of *Romans* (written 1916–1918, published 1919).

DIALECTICAL THEOLOGY

Dialectical theology is both a technical term for this particular period in Barth's life and also for the school of dialectical theology, describing the theological movement away from liberalism. How did Barth execute the turn from man-centredness to God-centredness? How did he execute this program of the primacy and centrality of God?

Forerunners
There were some precursors besides the Blumhardts. One was the famous philosopher of religion, Rudolf Otto, with his book *The Idea of the Holy* (1917, 2nd edition 1958). The book has been enormously popular. Otto said that in the world of religion the decisive element is not God as a continuation of the world of man, but the otherness of God, the transcendence of God. Such a pronouncement blocked the thrust of liberal theology. Otto even spoke of the irrational element in the idea of the divine. "God is the wholly other."

There was also one other gentlemen who anticipated Barth's work, less influential than Otto, but who had been the first to proclaim the necessity of a theocentric theology: Eric Schäder (one of Cremer's evangelical nuclei at Griefswald). In 1911, he published *Theocentric Theology*, a critique of nineteenth century theology, which he condemns as anthropocentric. But he lacked the charisma to be a great leader. The breakthrough only came with Karl Barth.

The Program
Dialectical theology emphasizes a theology of contrast, or antithesis. God is the *totaliter aliter*, the totally different.

But the term "dialectical" can mean many different things. It can mean dialogue, suggesting that the truth can only be found in the interweaving of the contributions of both parties to the dialogue. There are a number of people who believe that God can only be found in dialogue, with the contributions of different religions gathered together. That's one form of dialectic. Another, the most famous form in philosophy, is the Hegelian dialectic: we begin with a thesis, and then add to it its antithesis, its opposite. The two then merge into a synthesis, which in turn forms the thesis for the next level in an upward spiral of contributions of thought. Within the synthesis there are elements of both the thesis and the antithesis.

Barth's theology cannot, on either definition, be named "dialectical." The "dialectical" theologians had no desire to merge with liberalism, its opposite. Nor did they seek dialogue with liberals. They were vigorously hostile to liberalism, not seeking rapprochement with it. "Dialectical theology," rather, is a term slapped on them by some onlooker who didn't have his language right. In terms of actual content, Barth's theology might be called "dia-statical"—two stances—theology. Reconciliation was never Barth's intention.

Barth's first public reaction against the liberal harmonization of God and world was a paper in 1919 which he read at Tambach (a forested village in the heart of Germany, the site of one of the liberal theological rallies after the war). He was invited, because he had a social interest, to speak on the Christian in society. It was the first public opportunity to voice dissonance with ruling liberalism. He spoke of the "wholly other" in God (Rudolf Otto's term) which rejects all secularization. He challenged all accommodations to culture. The God of Scripture, he declared, has no room for all the hyphen theologies—Christian-social, religious-social, divine-human. God does not bring peace but unrest

Karl Barth (1886–1968)

into the world. God mounts a critical opposition to all human-centred activity. The negation, originating in God, of all things of this world is the only truly positive stance.

At that very same time, and without collaboration or even contact between the two men, Emil Brunner in Zürich rattled his sabre. He said the New Testament is not about humaneness (as the liberals said) but rather speaks of the limits of humaneness. God is the critic of all human efforts. A better term for the school of dialectical theology is "a theology of crisis." God is the crisis of man.

The theology of crisis marks a striking recurrence, in new guise, of the old negative theology. This has always been the alternative to a theology which glorifies the human, the natural and the rational as a way to arrive at God. Early Barth is a representative of that stream of theology going back to Martin Luther and Augustine. There may even be a direct line. Barth wrote the second edition of *Romans*—a theologically iconoclastic work—under the direct influence of the recently rediscovered *Lectures on Romans* by the young Martin Luther (1516).

The Execution of the Program

Barth executed the program of dialectical theology with the publication of the second edition of *Romans*. This was a completely different book from the first edition. As Barth wrote to a friend, it "left no stone unturned." It is not really a commentary on Romans so much as a manifesto of Barth's new theological stance.

It is the document of the theology of crisis. It was written in a creative explosion of ten or twelve months (like Schleiermacher's first book). He just ate, slept, wrote, and occasionally preached. He said, "My church didn't see much of its pastor" during those months.

It was unlikely that Barth should have written the second edition of *Romans* at all. Copies of the first edition had run out. The publisher asked Barth for notes to correct the first edition. Barth was uncertain. At that time, one of the heroes of the school of dialectical theology, Friedrich Gogarten (1887–1967), spent three days with Barth. Barth wrote to Thurneysen, "Gogarten was here for three days and we spoke three days and three nights. And now I know how I have to write the second edition of *Romans*." Gogarten must have told Barth about the recently discovered and published Luther lectures with their negative approach to culture.

That was the seminal idea in the second edition. The forward reveals the book's tone and tenor. Barth wrote, "If I have had one governing principle in this book, it is 'the infinite qualitative difference of time and eternity,'" (quoting Kierkegaard)—that is, the vast difference between God and man. "God is heaven and you are on earth" (Ecc. 5:2). It is a theology of antithesis. God is described as the overall negation, and even annihilation, of man and his world. No, Dr. Harnack, there is no point of contact between God and man. The worst thing is to think that there is. Religion, the human effort to reach God, is worse than atheism. Religious experience is the worst evil of all.

Here, we can see evangelicals coming into Barth's sights. To speak of religious experience, according to Barth, is high treason to the gospel. We have to do away with all psychology of religion and all history of religion, those pet subjects of the liberals. They have nothing to do with the real God. There is no point of contact. We have simply to believe, not to touch or to see or to experience. God is strictly and utterly transcendental.

A strong Kantianism, with its great divide between immanence and transcendence, is evident here. No communication takes place between the two sides, heaven and earth. Only Barth, in contrast to Kant, takes his position on the other side of the border, in the beyond. God is transcendent and that is where the theologian must have his footing.

Implications for the Incarnation

At this time, Barth had no room for the idea of incarnation. Jesus was the highest possibility of religious man. Therefore he had to fail. His crucifixion was the crucifixion of all religious attempts. What we have here is the most radical denial of what later became Barth's central concern: God's condescension, God's coming down, is God with us. God's becoming man is the central concern of the later Barth. But in early Barth, God is the negation of man, the undoing of all that man does.

Implications for Ethics

What does this mean for ethics? Romans 6 and Romans 12 compel Barth to discuss ethics. God's work, Barth says, only touches a person on the top of the head, like a tangent touches a circle. He explicitly denies all mystical experience of Christ within us.

God does not enter our life; he is transcendent. All the good works mentioned in Romans 6 and Romans 12 are to be understood in an eschatological sense, as a promise for the future. This is only promise, not event.

For Barth, the invisibility of God is a first principle. The term "invisibility," is almost the ruling phrase in the second edition of *Romans*. We cannot, he says, have any sense experience of God or of any effect of God. The quest for reality in some movements in Christianity would have sent the early Barth hissing and shouting: "Why demand to see what you're asked to believe?" So Barth destroys ethics. He subtitles Romans 12 "The Great Disturbance." His question: How can Paul, having said that God has done everything, allow that man should do anything? How can there be an eagerness for human activity in the New Testament if human works don't achieve anything and have no meaning? Why is there such an enormous amount of exhortation in the New Testament? It is paradoxical. Barth—ignoring all that New Testament exhortation—says conversion is a 360 degree turn. It is not reversing your direction. You continue in the same direction. "Do what you are doing anyway, only do it without that final commitment which you have had so far." Barth's pet verse was Colossians 3:3: "Your life is now hidden with Christ in God." All reality is above, not here on earth.

Thurneysen at that time wrote a little essay and drew the consequence which Karl Barth never expressed in so many words. Thurneysen said one step more or less in the direction of sin doesn't matter under the height of eternity. If the level of our living is so removed from God anyway, sin is inconsequential. This, as Bonhoeffer saw it, is a doctrine of justification, not of the sinner, but of sin.

This justification of sin became very clear in two addresses which Barth gave in 1926–1927. He was asked to speak at the annual summer meeting of the German Christian Student Association (equivalent to InterVarsity) on the Baltic coast. Being strong evangelicals and pietists, they were trying to work out their sanctification and live a life of discipleship. Barth gave two lectures which shook the movement for years. He attacked them unrelentingly for two or three days. He called their quest for sanctification pharisaical. If they had known the grace of God, he declared, they wouldn't be trying to sanctify themselves. There's no need for that. All is grace.

There is a rigid logic to all this. If God does everything, then it would be quite wrong for humans to do anything. This same logic is present in some of Martin Luther's students. They said it is far safer not to do good works. You might become proud and think that you have done something. That would be self-justification by works, and you would have fallen into the Roman Catholic trap, and then the Reformation was in vain. Good works are dangerous for salvation.

A story illustrates how Barth's thinking took hold. An Oxford professor of New Testament visited Denmark in the 1930s where Barthianism had strongly invaded the Lutheran church. This hyper-Lutheran attitude went right into the bloodstream of the Danish Lutheran churches. With the dangerous political scene and the war on the horizon, the Oxford professor spoke about the need for a moral change. A pastor in Copenhagen confessed not to understand a word of it. The pastor said if he went out and took a prostitute it wouldn't make the slightest difference in the light of eternity. It might even be better, because you would avoid the greatest sin, trying to be holy in God's eyes—that is self-righteousness, the worst possible sin.

This was the teaching that had gone deep into the fabric of the European churches. That great critic of Christianity Ludwig Feuerbach said that the strategy for eliminating Christianity was simple: first, get rid of the practice of Christianity. When that is gone, then the theory—the theology—will also go. Perhaps that explains the threadbare Christianity in Europe today. As much as we might admire and applaud Barth's heroic recovery of biblical Christianity in his later work, we must point out that much of the damage he later had to repair he himself caused in his early work.

THE MOVE TOWARD NEO-ORTHODOXY

Unlike his colleagues, Barth continued to change, being the first of them to move away from dialectical theology and on to neo-orthodoxy. That somebody should go back to study the dusty tomes of the seventeenth and eighteenth centuries was unheard of. He developed a position which may be called "theomonism." It came out clearly in *Christian Dogmatics I*

(1927, to be distinguished from the later *Church Dogmatics*; Barth abandoned the attempt after the first volume and started afresh in 1932). *Dogmatics I* contains prolegomena, as is usual for the first chapter of dogmatics. (Prolegomena deal with questions like knowledge of God, theological cognition, revelation, perhaps a doctrine of Scripture, the task of theology.) In 1922, in the second edition of *Romans*, Barth expounded the antithesis between God and man in terms of a negation of man. In 1927, he continued with the same antithesis in this first attempt at dogmatics, but now he emphasized the affirmation of God. The Kantianism and the otherworldliness remain, but the emphasis has shifted from a criticism of man to an affirmation of God. Whereas *Romans* (1922) proclaimed, "Man is nothing," *Christian Dogmatics* (1927) proclaimed, "God is everything." It is the same dialectic, only now Barth takes the other side of the dialectic. Another decisive turn for Barth occurred in 1930, which is the period in which he began the *Church Dogmatics*.

Comments on Dialectical Theology

(1) *The principality (or centrality) of God.* The turnaround from anthropocentric to theocentric theology, and the rejection of liberalism, came in 1916 with the first edition of *Romans* (not in 1922 as most people believe). The First Edition, far more than the Second, is of lasting relevance. Its message: Let God be God again (and not an extension of man). It was a return to giving God the glory, and not ourselves. This return to the centrality of God was decisive to overcoming liberalism at that time. That is a necessary step forward and must be retained.

The point might be buttressed with a little anecdote. I had a conversation with Karl Barth in 1963. He was retired and I was a twenty-five year-old teaching assistant at Basel with one of his colleagues in the field of ethics. It was a time

Karl Barth (1886–1968)

when liberalism was coming into another heyday. There had been fifteen years of Bultmann's rule in the universities, pushing Barth back into the shadows. Beyond that, the new liberalism was on the rampage. J. A. T. Robinson published *Honest to God*. It was a 128-page manifesto of modern liberalism. There was the new morality, and God defined as the "depth of being." Prayer was out and meditation was in. Barth by that time had become frustrated with the rule of the Bultmannian school. Barth and Bultmann had been colleagues in the 1920s and respected each other highly. But by the 1960s, Barth was becoming impatient and was calling the Bultmannian school the company of Korah—which ought to be swallowed by the earth (Num. 16).

Barth and I talked for two and a half hours about the contemporary situation. He asked what we had done wrong that 300,000 copies of Robinson's book in German should be devoured by the church. Copies of the blue lines were being sold under the counter. It was a real "ideological advance." Everybody knew what this book meant.

The atheist forces got together when the book came out. Robinson got a full hour on the BBC and a full page in the *Sunday Observer*. The same thing happened in Germany. To top it off, Karl Barth's own publishing house was the one that published Robinson. I expressed to Barth a longing for someone to do for this generation what he did for his, to rein in the liberalism which was running wild, to restore God's honour. In his seminar the year before, Barth had said that all theology is to glorify God. It is to do exactly what the Roman Catholic priest does in the mass when he elevates the elements. Theology must elevate God. But what, in fact, is it doing? It is only speaking about man in a louder voice. "We need," I said to Barth, "someone to do what you did."

Barth looked at me and answered in a grumbling tone: "You do it." He was right. We must all take responsibility for such a reversal, for a re-Christianization of theology.

We are in a similar situation as Barth was in 1915–1920. Twenty-five years ago, Jürgen Moltmann said the confessing church movement, and Barthianism in general, represented a return to the centre. It was a centripetal movement. We must now go out and recover the peripheries, the horizons: ethics, sociology, psychology. This has been done, and very successfully. But theologians, in becoming sociologists, psychologists, journalists, have too often left theology behind. One of the spokespersons of modern theology, Dorothy Sölle (professor at Union Theological Seminary and at Hamburg in Germany) said, "If Christ came back today, he would come with a submachine gun." In eschatology, we're often told that the kingdom of God is established through the work of our own hands. In my lifetime I have heard theologians say that in times of social and political crises, the question of God must be put on ice for a while. Others say the social and political questions of the day in fact comprise the God question. Sometimes such questions—and our politically correct responses to them—are made into a new confessionalism. A synod of the Reformed Church of Northwest Germany decided in the 1980s that one's position on unilateral disarmament determined whether that person is a Christian brother or not. Conversion, then, becomes the acceptance of a political stance. This is the classical reduction of the love of God to the love of neighbour: the centre has been lost. This severs relationship to the living God. Ironically, it also threatens love of neighbour by killing motivation for social involvement and ethical living. So our need again is to move toward the centre. In much of the writing of many "evangelicals" in North America, we glimpse the same trends: a centrifugal movement into religious philosophy or whatever. Both Robert Schuller and Robert Johnston say the theocentric must become the anthropocentric today.

Karl Barth (1886–1968)

Only when the sacred becomes secular can God work. So the topic is no longer God, but Humanity. In this theology, Jesus' humanity is of interest, but not his divinity. The cutting edge of theological reflection in North American evangelicalism has moved from the divine to the human. But how secular must we get before we return to a hunger for the sacred? Evangelicals rejected that centrifugal movement to the peripheries in the 1950s. They were still orthodox then. But with the traditional twenty to thirty year incubation period which evangelicals always require, they have jumped on the bandwagon. And so we need a new departure: like Barth in 1915.

(2) *The reality of God.* While Barth's first concern was the primacy of God, his second concern was the reality of God. Here, he fought a running battle throughout his life. And the task is yet unfinished. How do we, as well as establishing God's primacy, also safeguard and establish the reality of God and his works? In the second phase of Barth's theological biography, he was beginning to see a need for the primacy of God, but had not yet written his commentary on Romans and had not yet entered the phase of dialectical theology. In these four or five years (1916–1920), he came to understand the quest for the reality of God and God's works. It is exactly what his teacher Johann Christoph Blumhardt had emphasized. Blumhardt revived that rare sentiment of early pietism, a strong hope for a better time yet to come for the church militant here on earth. The future of the church will not be all dryness and defeat as at present, but we will see the reality of God's work through the Holy Spirit. If that takes place, there would be immediate implications for the doctrine of sanctification. There will be real changes in peoples' lives.

Good works would be evident (Matt. 5:16) "that everyone may see your progress" (1 Tim. 4:15). God's effects would be visible in a person's life. This has implications not only for the doctrine of sanctification for the individual but for the whole history of Christianity. Does Christianity make any difference to the course of history or doesn't it? Are there traces of the work of God in history? Is there something to be seen, evidence of renewal and change? When Barth began, he was very much in harmony with this thrust of Blumhardt's. Barth used a famous image in a lecture during this short time period. He said when he looks at the waves spreading in the pond of ancient history, he knows that the stone that produced the ripple—Christ—must have been huge. In saying that, Barth acknowledged the visibility of the effects of God's work. God is evident in the history of salvation.

Dialectical Theology: God's Works Invisible

However, when Barth moved into the period of dialectical theology (1921–1922) the whole question of the reality of God was shunned.

The postulate of the invisibility of God and his works recurs over and over in Barth's writing through this period. It is an invisibility of God on principle. He makes a sharp distinction between the confusion visible in the world and the invisible, transcendent world. Belief in this world demands pure faith, "naked faith." There's nothing to be seen. At this stage, Barth claims, "History is provably empty of God." God's work is strictly a matter of faith in the invisible and the transcendent. What we have here is a vast apologetic (in the sense of defensive) move, a move of withdrawal. Barth pulls back from the world of the scientists: the physical world, the historical world, the psychological world, the philosophical world. He evacuates all areas under siege, and removes Christian truth into transcendence, where presumably it is safe. This is only a Platonic version of the Kantian scheme we saw earlier. Kant, too, established an antithesis between the immanent and the transcendent.

Karl Barth (1886–1968)

There was no way to move from one sphere to another. The school of dialectical theology maintains that antithesis, only it puts all the theological content into transcendence. The real truth is in the beyond—a Platonic solution.

Response to the "Invisibility" of God's Works

But this is a severe redefinition of Christian faith. Is Christianity the religion of faith in the invisible? All the dialectical theologians emphasized John 20:29: "Because you have seen me, you have believed; blessed are those who have not seen and yet have believed." But what is faith? Is it a faith in the invisible? On the one hand, faith is the same thing as confidence and hope. Hebrews 11:7 and 11 speaks of Noah's faith concerning events as yet unseen. The object of faith is not a certain state of things in invisible transcendence but something which lies in the future. Faith is related not so much to transcendence as to the future. "By faith Noah, when warned about things not yet seen, in holy fear built an ark to save his family." The same is true of Abraham. "By faith Abraham, when called to go to a place he would later receive as his inheritance, obeyed and went" (Heb. 11:8). Faith here is looking forward, not upward. Strangely enough, the same is true of the Old Testament verse (Hab. 2:4) which for him is the central verse on faith: "But the righteous will live by his faith," which Paul quotes in Romans 1:17. The context in Habakkuk points to a future time. For example:

> For the revelation awaits an appointed time;
> it speaks of the end
> and will not prove false.
> Though it linger, wait for it;
> it will certainly come and will not delay.
> (Hab. 2:3)

That is the situation for faith. Something has been promised but has not yet arrived. Faith as confidence always covers the intermediate time between promise and fulfilment, and always has to be strictly related to that. Faith, therefore, is related to events. That is faith as hope.

Faith has another meaning in Scripture. It looks back to events in the history of salvation. So faith is both hope and remembrance. Jesus chides his disciples for having little faith because they do not remember. "Do you still not understand? Don't you remember the five loaves for the five thousand, and how many basketfuls you gathered? Or the seven loaves for the four thousand, and how many basketfuls you gathered?" (Matt. 16:9–10). They feared in their present situation because they had no bread. Or, after Jesus walks on the water (Mk. 6:52), "They were completely amazed, for they had not understood about the loaves; their hearts were hardened." Psalm 77:12 declares:

> I will meditate on all your works
> and consider all your mighty deeds.

So faith, biblically understood, is rooted in event, both past and future. Compared with this, the faith of dialectical theology is ontological. It is an a-historical faith. It relates not to event but to present transcendence. As a result, dialectical theology depicts not a moral cleavage between man and God but an ontological one. Man is separated from God by ontological otherness, not by sin. On this understanding, sanctification, defined as the practice of holy living, falls by the wayside.

This means that dialectical theology says just the opposite of what Barth was beginning to say under the influence of Blumhardt. According to dialectical theology, there is no visible fruit of sanctification. We don't live differently; we only view ourselves differently—as forgiven sinners. This

Karl Barth (1886–1968)

is what the Bultmannians preach to the present day: in regeneration we begin to see ourselves in a different light. We don't change our lifestyle.

For Barth at this time, sanctification is strictly a matter of faith. Nothing changes outwardly. I only believe that I am a different person in the eyes of God. The consequence for Christian ethics is that there is no distinction between good and evil here on earth. That famous German proverb applies here: "In the night all the cats are grey." In the night of this world, where the sun of transcendence is so far removed, there's not much difference between wickedness and virtue. Karl Heim said Barth here teaches the common shipwreck of humanity. When the whole ship goes down, individual folly or heroism, righteousness or sin, means nothing.

Barth overdoes the negation of man. Man stands under ontological accusation, not, as in the New Testament, under moral accusation. But a mere ontological understanding of humanity's separation from God destroys the concept of sin, and with it the necessity of justification.

Summary of the Critique of Dialectical Theology

There is a keen irony to dialectical theology: the attempt to destroy humanism in order to return to God-centredness has been taken into human hands. There may be truth in the observation that there is a relationship between dialectical theology and the mystical medieval *theologia negativa*, where the glory of God is safeguarded by the annihilation of man. Both are warped versions of a legitimate concern, theocentricity. Both programs were executed in defective fashion: the denial of man, with the assertion of God over against man, became mere mechanism, a knee jerk. We can say, in summary, "Yes" to the dialectical theologian's insistence on the primacy of God. But we must say "No" to their Platonic view of the reality of God.

CHRISTOMONISM

The year 1931 marked a new departure for Barth. In that year, Barth published *Anselm: Fides Quaerens Intellectum (Faith Seeks Understanding)*. It is on Anselm's ontological proof for the existence of God, a book on the old problem of the relationship between faith and reason. It is a small book, and different from all his other books. It is a monograph, a historical treatise. If Barth had ever done a doctorate (which the very great don't need to do), this would have been his thesis. But of course by that time he already had one or two honourary doctorates.

Anselm of Canterbury had said, "God is that compared with which nothing higher can be thought." According to Anselm, this means that God must necessarily have the quality of existence. Otherwise we could think of an entity greater than God which had all the divine attributes plus the quality of existence. The ontological argument can be distilled to this: "perfection exists." If something is absolutely perfect, it must also have the quality of existence.

This famous argument for the existence of God has determined the philosophy of religion for eight hundred years. Karl Barth, innovative as ever, turns the whole thing around. He says this formula was far from being a philosophical definition. No. Rather, it is obvious that the phrase "God is that compared with which nothing higher can be thought" comes from the liturgy, from worship. It is not a philosophical proof. It is prayer! Faith is presupposed. Anselm isn't arguing somebody into faith, but is simply adoring the God in whom he has already put his faith. So Barth turned the whole history of the interpretation of this argument upside down. It is not a theological argument to establish God's existence. It is reason following faith.

Barth's revolutionary reinterpretation of Anselm had enormous consequences for his own theology, from the

Karl Barth (1886–1968)

1930s on. Faith and revelation always came first, knowledge and reason second. It meant the end of all philosophical underpinnings of theology. It meant the removal of all natural theology. He would have nothing to do with natural theology as an introduction to faith. Barth resolutely does away with the arguments for the existence of God.

Barth's major emphasis which grew out of his understanding of the priority of faith was that "faith" is *faith in Christ*. Therefore, all theology must be Christology. We have labelled this concentration "Christomonism." Barth would disown that label, but it sticks nonetheless. Barth's whole development in this area is expressed in his *Church Dogmatics*, the first volume of the first part which was published in 1932. His dogmatics do not begin with the doctrine of man or natural revelation, but with the Word of God in Christ as the first principle of all dogmatics. Of course, the other renewal here is that Barth calls his work "church" dogmatics. From now on, Barth purposely relates theology to the sphere of the church. He is consciously serving the church, which is revolutionary in itself.

Christomonism and "faith first" (followed by understanding or reason) meant for Barth the disruption of fellowship with most of his close colleagues of dialectical theology. Brunner, Bultmann, and Gogarten went the opposite way. They were trying to find a point of contact for faith in the natural world. Brunner's 1934 book was called *Nature and Grace*, picking up on the traditional formula.

Karl Barth's thesis is applied in a series of lectures given in 1933. One of these is titled "The First Commandment as Theological Axiom." The title might have indicated Barth's rediscovery of the primacy of God, but what he really intended here was to discard all natural theology. For him, natural theology now meant to have other gods. He began to denounce anyone speaking of revelation apart from Christ. He had no mercy for talk of "creational ordinances" or "creational order" or "general revelation." This is a return to his life's theme: let God be God. But it is a strange execution of that theme, a very narrow interpretation of it.

Barth's next step was to publish his small monograph *Theological Existence Today!* (1933). The enormous, almost providential, fruitfulness and applicability of his negation of natural theology became evident on January 20, 1933 when the National Socialists (Nazis) took over. Their rise to power was held out to be a national revolution, a renewal of self-esteem. The German people were rising up in pride again. There was a boundless self-confidence. The third empire, *das Dritte Reich*, had begun. (The first was the Holy Roman Empire of the German nation which was dissolved in 1804 after lasting almost a thousand years. The second was the reunification of Germany in 1871.) The "third empire" had enormous eschatological overtones. Joachim de Fiore (c. 1135–1202), the heterodox abbot in the 12th century in Italy, spoke of three empires (of Father, Son, and Holy Spirit). It was thought to last a thousand years. The millennium was the third Reich. Hitler, calling his own state the "third Reich," implied it would last a thousand years (the National Socialist millennium lasted, in fact, twelve). This remarkable development in 1934 was supported by a group which soon became the strongest party in the Protestant church, the "German Christians." The German Christians, an arm of the National Socialists, were at the point of taking over the Protestant churches altogether. Their famous phrase was, "Germany our aim, Christ our strength." The German Christians saw Hitler as God's hand in history acting for his people. Therefore, German Christians must completely redress the life and structure of the church according to the principles of National Socialism. Jesus was the great Führer. Of course, this restructuring meant that they did away with the Old Testament, that "terrible Jewish book."

Karl Barth (1886–1968)

This was the vindication of Barth's rejection of natural theology. Natural theology tried to see God both in nature and history. But look what that produced: Christians who follow Hitler. Barth rejected the idea that God's hand is revealed in history, especially in the places where we personally wanted it most. Barth's battle against this view of history took the form of his fight against natural theology. The battle began, we have seen, with the publication of a small book, *Theological Existence Today!*, which was written on the 24th and 25th of June, 1933, half a year into the most turbulent time for National Socialism. In it, Barth warns against forgetting the exclusive and primary demand of God's Word. We must hear his word before and over the many urgent demands of the day. He writes:

> There are some things about which there is unanimity with the church. One is that there is no more urgent demand in the whole world than that which the Word of God makes, that is the Word of God to be preached and heard. Therefore even in the turbulent demands of the day, with all those many urgencies which are being pressed upon us, we need to continue to do theology as if nothing had happened.

That task would be the same yesterday and today. The equivalent of what Barth did would be somebody standing up today in Bosnia and saying, "The most urgent thing is not territorial claims, not war, and not peace, but to listen to the Word of God." It took sheer courage for Barth publish such a book at that time. It was a prophetic contribution and of lasting relevance, a word of warning that we must never replace the primacy of God with the primacy of anything else.

In May 1934, the Christian struggle against the National Socialists reached a new pitch. Barth and others called for a confessing synod, the famous Barmen synod (Barmen is an industrial city in the Rhineland). This synod became the focus of resistance. Barth said, "It is not the task of the church to discover and proclaim God in the events of the day." God is not, as has sometimes been claimed by the World Council of Churches, "where the action is." Barth, contrary to that sentiment, declared, "Jesus Christ is the only Word of God that we have to hear," and the church does not listen to any other voice.

Barth also broke with Brunner in the fall of 1934 over this issue. Brunner had written *Nature and Grace* in order to establish a point of contact, of discussion, with philosophy and other areas of inquiry. He said that dialectical theology was too negative and argued that we needed to be more interdisciplinary. Brunner said that he didn't claim that there was an image of God left in man after the fall in terms of any substance, but there is still something like a formal image of God left in man: his answerability.

Barth answered Brunner with his sixty page pamphlet *No!* He accused Brunner of committing the age-old heresy of natural theology, and he found it particularly unwise of Brunner to publish this renewed search for natural theology at that moment in history: it would only support the claim of the German Christians that they, by way of natural theology, saw Hitler as God's hand in history. Barth was furious in his reproach.

THE NEW LOOK OF ETHICS

Gospel and Law

Barth in his *Dogmatics* also introduced a new ethics. In 1934, Barth refused to swear an oath to Hitler and so was dismissed from his position. Being Swiss, he was able to return to Basel. In 1935, just before he left Germany, he was invited to address a large church gathering, again

Karl Barth (1886–1968)

at Barmen. He came up with another very innovative approach, *Gospel and Law*, parallel to his reversal of faith and knowledge in 1931. Both Lutheranism and Calvinism see the traditional sequence as law and gospel: first the law reveals our sinfulness, then the gospel holds out the remedy. This traditional approach appears to derive from the structure of the book of Romans. Up to Romans 3:20, Paul demonstrates our guilt through the law. From then on, he proclaims God's forgiveness through the gospel. So law first, to convict the sinner, and then gospel, to preach forgiveness and justification. This same order was embodied in the traditional "three uses" of the law in Reformational orthodoxy: *usus politicus* (the use of the law in the civil law); *usus elenchticus* (from a Greek word used in the pastorals which means "accusation," used for the criminal law and within the church for the use of the law in the conviction of sin); *usus in renatis* (the use of the law in the life of the regenerate). These are built on the sequence of law and gospel. The gospel is the answer to the conviction of sin produced by the accusing use of the law. But Barth turns this around. He says the gospel comes first, then the law.

What does this mean for the traditional "three uses" of the law? Barth reduces the three uses of the law to the third use, for the regenerate. This third use is also strongly represented in Calvinism, whereas Lutheranism emphasizes the accusing use of the law. Barth's position is of major importance. He virtually does away with the first two uses of the law. What then creates conviction of sin? Not the commandments, but the gospel. The law, Barth said, can bring only superficial repentance. But in Christ's cross, sinners see their sinfulness. Here, the gospel accuses before it offers forgiveness and liberation. Some of Barth's followers have taken this idea in the direction of antinomianism. There is gospel, and gospel, but no law. But Barth never said that. He emphasized the commandments, but put them in second place.

Lutherans have pointed out a flaw in Barth's position: if the gospel is used both ways, to accuse and to forgive, when does it accuse, and when does it forgive? Is the message of God's forgiveness and love to be spoken to those who are still in the depths of their pride? Surely they need to be shaken by the law. Such people are fortified in their rebellion against God. The preacher who begins with gospel is like the lifeguard at a beach on a beautiful day who throws life preservers at people. They don't see themselves in any danger, so why bother grabbing hold? We must, the Lutherans contend, make clear what people need to be saved from if we are ever to make justification plausible.

Barth argues for his position from the structure of the ten commandments. There, the message of salvation is first: "I am the Lord your God who brought you out of Egypt" (Deut. 5:6). Clearly, Barth is correct on this point. So there emerges two possible arrangements: both law and gospel, and gospel and law. Both are legitimate. They apply to different situations in the church. If it is a preliminary preaching of the gospel, it should be gospel, then law, as when Israel was liberated from Egypt. But in the prophets, who addressed a people who had fallen from grace, we see the order reversed. They accuse the nation of Israel and promise salvation only after they have turned back. Our own situation—a formerly Christian civilization lapsed into neo-paganism, humanism, atheism—is closer to that which prevailed around the time of the prophets. The sequence for our time, then, is law, then gospel.

Barth was both right and wrong. The gospel indeed creates a conviction of sin in terms of motivation. The suffering of Christ can motivate a person far more deeply than any encounter with the ten commandments. But in terms of the subject matter of sin, what sin is, the ten commandments guide us. The cross of Christ explains the "that" of sin but the commandments continue to explain the "what" of sin.

The New Social Ethics

What can Christocentrism say to social ethics? If the first use of the law (that is, in the criminal law of the land) has been abandoned and there is to be no more application of the law at the political and social level, what happens to social ethics? Are Christians to make a contribution? In 1938, Barth published his next treatise, *Justification and Justice*, showing the social ethical consequences of his reversal of law and gospel into gospel and law. The book's title is programmatic. Christ, the realm of redemption, comes first, and the realm of creation (where social justice takes place) takes its cue from what happens in Christ in justification. The program is to create a social ethics by setting out from faith, even setting out from Christology. This program has been called Christocracy, the rule of Christ both in society and the church.

What Barth does here is to take the principle of analogy, which is so pivotal for natural theology, and turn it around. Analogy in natural theology always moves upward. We have some knowledge; God has all knowledge, omniscience. We have some strength; God has all strength, omnipotence. It is ana-logy, a speaking upwards (the *analogia entis*, the analogy of being, beginning with being). Barth says we have to turn that around. Barth's analogy is downward. It begins with God and is applied to us. He calls it the *analogia fidei*, the analogy of faith. The traditional meaning of the "analogy of faith" was in hermeneutics (understanding an obscure passage by comparing it with other passages in Scripture and through the church creeds). Barth's position is more accurately called *akatalogy*, a speaking downwards.

Barth develops the principle of analogy in his next little book, *The Christian Community and the Civil Community* (1946). Here Barth says these two communities are like two circles which surround the same centre, which is Christ. Church and state have one focus, Christ. This is an image from Augustine. Barth says we have to begin with Revelation 22, the future heavenly city. We have to analogize downwards from there to the church and then, in a secondary analogy, from the church to the state. The church must be shaped according to the heavenly city. Then the state must be shaped by the church—"on earth as it is in heaven" (Matt. 6:10).

This means state officials become *ministeri extraordinari ex ecclesiae*, extraordinary ministers of the church. This has been called the Christocratic model for social ethics, as opposed to the traditional two kingdom concept of social ethics—where both church and state are under God, but each has a different set of rules. Christ, in Barth's proposal, is the standard for the state through the mediation of the church. Barth virtually proposes here a new clericalism. He has recaptured the medieval stance that the state is dependent on the church and the church tells the state how to behave.

There is another consequence of Christocracy. In a Christocracy—where Christ is the ruler of the state—the Sermon on the Mount would be the law of the land. Of course, no Christocentric theologian ever goes this far. But underlying such a theology is the secret assumption that salvation is universal, everybody is redeemed. Otherwise, the moral claims Christ makes cannot be placed on everyone. Today, in social ethics, this same idea of Christocracy, this Barthian idea of the kingdom of Christ in society, has replaced anticipation of the eschaton. The philosophy is "swords into plowshares" (Is. 2:4; Mic. 4:3). We must anticipate the coming down of the New Jerusalem (Rev. 21) and, using the Sermon on the Mount to guide us, structure society accordingly.

But, in objection to this, we must point out that Revelation 21 excludes the idea of a universalism, the applicability of the New Jerusalem to everybody. Revelation 21:27 says that the city is only open to those whose names are written in the Lamb's book of life: "Nothing impure will ever enter it, nor will anyone who does what is shameful or deceitful, but only those whose names are written in the Lamb's book of life." Scripture contradicts Barth's position.

Practically speaking, though, Barth's solutions in terms of politics were actually realistic and moderate. He ended up with a defense of exactly the kind of democracy in place in Switzerland. It is somewhat humorous that after all his analogizing he ended up with something that was already in place. Barth, we saw, insisted always that faith comes first and only then understanding, even in social ethics. But Barth admitted (probably with a smile) that Rousseau, with the natural light of reason, had seen the same things that he had. There is, however, a serious contradiction here to Barth's whole system. How could Rousseau arrive where Barth did with only the natural light of reason and without the revelation in Christ? Barth wrote and taught all his life to rule out such a possibility.

A further criticism has been made of Barth's whole system of analogizing. Analogies are treacherous. The analogy principle is a blank check for arbitrariness. The one who analogizes chooses the analogies and tailors them to fit his own creed or convictions. Barth's critics—especially the Lutherans—asked why he didn't advocate monarchy. If the state is to be shaped according to the church, should not it be a monarchy? Of course, Barth did nothing of the kind. He correctly argued for Swiss military defense against expanding German militarism (which threatened just across the river in Basel). But such an argument was made at the cost of the essential defencelessness of the church: what of the heavenly city which comes down without gates? God's city doesn't need to be defended.

And there was more. Barth, in line with his defense against Hitler's expansionist ambitions, once again contradicted his whole system of social ethics. In 1938, he wrote a famous letter to Josef Hromadka, a professor of theology in Prague, Czechoslovakia. (Hromadka later became famous as leader of the Christian Peace Conference, a pro-Soviet popular front.) When the Nazis began to occupy Czechoslovakia, Barth said that every Czech soldier fighting Hitler was a soldier of Christ. Here lies bare some of the contradictions of the Christocracy approach. The whole question of the appropriate model for doing Protestant social ethics is still up in the air.

THE LATER YEARS

Political Views

During the war, Barth was loudly anti-fascist. He was one of the most vocal spokesmen against Hitler in Switzerland. This took great courage because at any moment the Nazis could have absorbed Switzerland, Switzerland being only a little island surrounded by the axis powers. After the war, Barth's leanings to the left became unmistakable. He publicly dissociated Stalin and Hitler and had nothing to say about the 1956 Soviet suppression of the Hungarian uprising. He frequently associated with groups which, it was later revealed, were inspired by Moscow. His friends organized the Prague Christian Peace Conference, the agency for Christian pro-Soviet attitudes. However, in the *Letters 1961–1968*, Barth appears much less infatuated with, and much more critical of, these leftist associations. He reveals his struggles with his friends in the Christian peace movement. We can glimpse here a deeper meaning in the

Karl Barth (1886–1968)

fact that Barth never went to Prague or spoke at any of the peace conferences.

Selected Further Topographical Monographs

In 1941, Barth published a revolutionary monograph on the doctrine of baptism. In Barth's church, and in all the Reformational churches, it was an article of faith that infants be baptized. But Barth came out in favour of believer's baptism. The churches were aghast. He again treated this theme in the last volume of *Church Dogmatics*. Baptism is not a gift of God, he says, but the first act of obedience by the believer. It is an act of commitment and witness. He describes baptism in a form in which self-baptism would be the ideal.

In 1953, he wrote a book on Rudolf Bultmann. It is a bridge-building book, and irenic. But as we see from the *Letters 1961–1968*, he was mad at the Bultmannians. We mentioned that he called them "the curse of Korah which ought to be swallowed by the earth" (Num. 16).

In 1956, Barth published, coinciding with the bicentennial of the birth of Wolfgang Amadeus Mozart, his unexpected little book *Mozart*. Barth poured out his utter admiration and love for him. If there is an *anima naturaliter Christiana*, a naturally Christian soul (Tertullian's phrase), it is, Barth said, Mozart. His music is heavenly, something like a (natural?) revelation. Barth's view that before Mozart there was nothing in music earned him some enemies. It hurt all the evangelicals who thought that Bach is the final revelation in music. Then he hurt everybody else when he said there is really nothing after Mozart.

In 1966 Barth took a strong interest in the development of the Roman Catholic church. He may have done more than anyone outside the Catholic church to make the reforms of Vatican II, which really reflects his previous work, possible. Although invited as an observer at the council, he did not attend. But in 1966, he visited Rome and discussed its results with some of the leading cardinals. *Ad limina apostolorum (To the Limits of the Apostles)* contains his questions. He also had an acquaintance with Hans Küng (who wrote his doctoral dissertation on Barth's doctrine of justification, trying to prove that this foremost Protestant was fully Catholic orthodox). The *Letters 1961–1968* contain long letters of warning to Hans Küng not to confuse reformation of the Catholic church with Protestant liberalism. Karl Barth even then saw the direction in which Küng was going. After Barth's death, Küng went further in the direction of what is clearly traditional Protestant liberalism and became a Schleiermacherian. Küng was chucked out of his chair in theology and now teaches in the faculty of philosophy. Barth saw that Küng was mistaking Protestant liberalism for true Scriptural reformation.

THE *CHURCH DOGMATICS*

Structure

During the political turmoil of the 1930s and during the resulting war, Barth sat in Basel just on the other side of the Rhine from Germany. There was always the possibility of air attack or invasion, but he continued to produce the voluminous tomes of his *Church Dogmatics*. There are five overall parts to the *Dogmatics*. Part One (Volume I) is the Prolegomena. Prolegomena (Greek, "things that are said first") is a technical term for the theory of theological cognition. Traditionally the prolegomena contains something on natural theology and proofs for the existence of God—though not in Barth's *Dogmatics*—special revelation, the authority of Scripture, and the nature of theology. Barth also has something on the task of dogmatics and the Word of God and revelation. Part Two (Volume II) is the doctrine of God. Part Three (Volume III) is the doctrine of creation. Part Four (in several volumes) is the doctrine of reconciliation (what others would call soteriology), where Barth also deals with sin, the person and work of Christ, justification, sanctification, vocation, the church, and the Holy Spirit. Part Five, on the doctrine of redemption, was never written. Here we see a strange choice of vocabulary (also found in Schleiermacher). By "redemption," Barth means the eschatological consummation of salvation.

There are, then, five volumes, and several sub-volumes. Part Three, for example, the doctrine of creation, is a whole library of four sub-volumes. Part Four is broken down even further. IV/3 was such a big book that the publisher demanded that it be broken up into two sub-sub-volumes. The *Dogmatics* grew constantly. At the beginning, a chapter is a chapter. Later, a chapter is a volume. After that, a chapter is two or three volumes. At this rate, if there had been anything on the doctrine of redemption, a chapter might have filled a library.

The Structure of Each Part

The structure does not follow the traditional (17th century) division of systematic theology into dogmatics and ethics. Barth rejects that. He claimed that dogmatics and ethics could not be done independent of each other. To separate them, Barth claimed, spells disaster for theology, so he brings them back together. Each section of dogmatics, therefore, except in the Prolegomena, is followed by a treatment of the respective ethics. For example, the last chapter in *Volume II: The Doctrine of God*, is the first treatment on ethics, "God's Commandment." Similarly, the last chapter in *Volume III* is an ethics of creation, "The Commandment of the Creator" (that is, respect for life, marriage, vocation, and use of time). IV/4 has an ethics of reconciliation, special Christian ethics. (But here we have only fragments; Barth was getting too old to write.)

Barth began his specifically Christian ethics with baptism. He viewed baptism as an act of man, not an act of God. Baptism is not something that God does—the mediation of grace—but rather is the first act of obedience on the part of the believer.

We do have further lecture fragments which were edited after Barth's death. In them, we can glimpse the shape of the remaining ethics. After beginning with baptism, Barth would have structured the rest of Christian ethics as an exposition of the Lord's Prayer. His principle was in accordance with *Lex orandi est lex credendi et agendi* (the rule of prayer is also the rule of belief and action). We only have his exposition of the first three petitions of the Lord's Prayer. He would have followed it up with an exposition of the ethics of the eucharist. So baptism, Lord's Prayer, and eucharist would have made up his ethics of reconciliation. The chapter on ethics in V/4 might have been an exposition of how Christians behave in the eschaton, the last days.

Volume IV represents a very elaborate structure in itself. Barth was on a holiday and had a dream one night in which he saw the structure for *Volume IV* (Christology). He structured it in a traditional way, according to Calvin's *munus triplex*, the three-fold offices of Christ: priest, king, prophet. (Calvin's order was prophet, priest, and king.) Then he took the different doctrines—Christology, sin, soteriology, ecclesiology (the Holy Spirit and the church), and pneumatology (the Holy Spirit and the individual)— and tried to fit them into a matrix with the offices of Christ. The structure is good, but not compelling. It is very elaborate. And some of it is arbitrary: why is pride discussed in connection with Christ's priesthood and sloth with his kingship? What the structure does is force Barth to find three sections for each of Christology, sin, soteriology, ecclesiology and pneumatology.

Karl Barth (1886–1968)

Each chapter, however, is beautifully laid out, and a lot of new perspectives emerge. For example, one of the particular achievements within this system is Barth's enlargement of soteriology. Everybody else ended their discussion of this doctrine after exploring justification and sanctification. But Barth says sanctification is not an end, but a preparation for the third thing, vocation. Soteriology can only be properly understood if we understand that God saves a person in order to call that person, to give that person the vocation of being co-witness with Jesus. This is a revolutionary development. Soteriology does not end with justification and sanctification. The purpose of sanctification is for the believer to become a witness. Barth, in other words, defined the purpose of the Christian life, which was an enormous advance.

Theological Method in the Church Dogmatics

(1) *Method in general: analogy.* In Barth's *Church Dogmatics,* Christomonism is gradually replaced by Christocentrism. Christ is in the centre but is no longer the only concern. Barth gathers in again all the material of theology. He replaces the previous dominating principle of dialectical theology, the antithesis of God and man, or diastasis, with the principle of analogy. As mentioned before, this is not the traditional analogy principle of natural theology, *analogia entis* (the analogy of being, analogizing upwards from man) but an analogy that moves downward, *analogia fidei*— the analogy of faith. First we speak about God and about Christ in God, and then we can speak about the nature of man. It is a thinking downward, a katalogy. Christ is the principle which sets the analogy. Man is secondary. God and Christ in heaven are primary. Barth, therefore, does not teach a doctrine of man from a study of human biology or sociology or philosophy, as was traditional in theology (see III/2 for Barth's anthropology). Rather, Barth begins

with that phrase from the Nicene Creed describing Christ as *vere homo*, truly man. We learn about man from looking at Christ, the true man.

But there is a difficulty here. In some ways, Christ was not typical of every human being. For one thing, Christ never married. And Christ did not spend the whole of his life in a trade or a profession. Christ never followed up the natural creational human impulse to build a home. We do not get immediate instruction from the person of Christ on the relationship to possessions or on the relationship with the opposite sex. It is quite an undertaking to read everything of human nature from Christ.

The same difficulties are apparent in Barth's doctrine of the church. The same principle of analogizing downward is prominent here. Barth believes that the relationship of a husband and wife has to be deduced from the relationship of Christ and his church, and so he builds a system on Paul's marriage analogy in Ephesians 5. The church, Barth said, grew out of the death of Christ while he was in the grave, just as God made Eve from Adam's rib while he was asleep. But this is a specious analogy. Out of it, Barth was able to find out all kinds of things about human nature which simply are not found in Scripture. Analogies—we must say this again—are arbitrary, even if Paul used them.

The most important critique of Barth's methodology is this: analogy is a divisive tool. Analogy separates heaven and earth. The analogy is only a formal link between two entities. There is an analogy between myself and a photograph of myself, but the photograph has no life. The analogy principle does nothing to ascertain the reality of the analogical. The principle of analogy fails to bridge the antithesis between the two objects being compared. Also, analogy remains a purely intellectual movement—a conjuring of the mind, or an invention of language, a language event. And so analogy is, in some ways, the direct opposite of incarnation.

Karl Barth (1886–1968)

Incarnation is "enfleshment," not "enpicturement." Thus, the principle of analogy furthers the rule of Platonism in theology. In a sense, the analogy principle, in an attempt to emphasize the reality of God, has emphasized the unreality of man: man becomes merely an idea.

(2) *Analogy, Platonism and the doctrine of salvation.* Platonism is also evident in Barth's doctrine of salvation. There is a theocentricity here (in reaction to liberalism) which almost excludes man. Barth's hostility to the concept of religious experience, which we saw in him during the 1920s, continues. Regeneration is not an experience, but took place solely on Golgotha. The new life of the Christian is to be believed, not experienced. As in dialectical theology, the pet passage is Colossians 3:3: "For you died, and your life is now hidden with Christ in God."

(3) *Analogy, Platonism, and the doctrine of sanctification.* The same is true in Barth's section on sanctification. He writes, "Christ is sanctified for us. God's work of salvation takes place in a great height above us." We are only asked to look up and gaze at what has happened in Christ. Barth even goes so far as to turn Hebrews 12:1–2 on its head: "Therefore, since we are surrounded by such a great cloud of witnesses, let us throw off everything that hinders and the sin that so easily entangles, and let us run with perseverance the race marked out for us. Let us fix our eyes on Jesus . . . ." Barth only quotes the looking up to Jesus, but conceals the main verb in that passage, "let us run." There is no moral progress in the life of a person. There is not only a substitutionary justification, but a substitutionary sanctification, and even a substitutionary conversion. It is all in Christ. The Christian just has to believe it is true. Barth would say that God's work of conversion and sanctification only creates eddies in a stream. The stream churns for a moment, but always continues in the same direction.

(4) *Analogy, Platonism, and the doctrine of the church.* There is also a strong Platonism in Barth's doctrine of the church. He has a beautiful analysis of what the church is. The church is a "fellowship of witness," a "fellowship of prayer," and a "fellowship of life" where believers share their life together. It is a compelling portrait.

But its flaw can be illustrated by a personal story. When I was about three or four months into my first pastorate, one quiet Sunday afternoon I thought it would be a good idea to reread what Barth had learned about the church and to see whether I was on the right track in the work I had begun. It was edifying to see his description of the church. How marvellous, how rich! Then, I turned the page wondering how to get there. But there was only half a page. Barth describes, he says, only what God knows his church to be. It is, simply, to be believed: man should never try to implement it with his dirty hands. The church as God knows it cannot be experienced. The Platonism here is plain: the "real church" is in heaven, in God's mind. The earthly church is just a shadow.

(5) *Analogy, Platonism, and revelation.* What does this Platonism mean in terms of the doctrine of revelation? As we have seen, the antithesis here is between analogy and incarnation (or condescension). In the *Church Dogmatics,* Barth gives the traditional doctrine of the divine decrees a new significance. The traditional doctrine of the divine decrees said that God, before creation, decreed what his work would be. In Barth's system, the whole salvation story seems to be removed to, almost reduced to, the decrees of God. This concept is central for Barth, just as it is in the Reformed orthodox doctrine of election. The whole salvation story is removed into the mind of God. Earthly realization is almost superfluous. This is a theological parallel to Platonic idealism: salvation is not so much an act of God as an idea of God, complete, beautifully elaborate, no detail

missing. Barth gives the richest dogmatics imaginable, but it is all in the mind of God, removed from earthly reality. It is also, conveniently, removed from historical criticism. So here we have a theology which is secretly determined by the dictates of the Enlightenment. The material of theology is not internalized this time but transcendentalized. The question is whether there is not secretly something at work here which is quite comparable to Bultmann's existentialization of the gospel. Both are trying to get away from the stranglehold of historical criticism. Barth's theology may be a restatement of another man's answer to the Enlightenment, that of Bishop George Berkeley (1685–1753) in Britain. Berkeley also responded to the Enlightenment with a transcendentalization of the content of revelation. There is a tendency in Barth to reduce revelation to the decrees of God, plus perhaps the verbal communication of those decrees to humanity. God's decision that his Son is to be incarnate is sufficient. The actual incarnation is a kind of afterthought, almost unnecessary. Martin Luther had a quite different idea of the decrees of God. In his commentary on Genesis, Luther said God was like a man who speaks to himself (the decrees) and then speaks aloud and things begin to happen:

> For he spoke, and it came to be;
> he commanded, and it stood firm. (Ps. 33:9)

(6) *Analogy, Platonism, and the doctrine of sin.* What does this principle of analogy and Platonism do to the doctrine of sin (III/3)? Barth's strong Platonic idealism leads practically to the annihilation of sin. Barth joins a famous tradition in the history of Christian theology which describes sin as non-being. Although it may be active and actual, it has no real being. It is only the lack of the good. This is also a Platonic postulate. Evil is something, but it is not being; therefore,

it is not real. The theological rule of thumb behind this is *ens at bonum convertuntur* (whatever is, is good). Being and good are synonyms. The biblical ground for it comes from the phrase in Genesis 1:31, where what God creates he also names as good. Thus, the bad is what God has not created. But this results in a description of sin as an "impossible possibility" (Barth's phrase), or to use Marx's phrase in his criticism of Plato, "sin is an existing untruth." It should not exist, but it exists. The tradition from Plato runs through Thomas Aquinas (who also has the view that evil is only a lack of the good, a deficiency of good but not something in itself), and Schleiermacher (Karl Barth's great enemy), and into Barth. "Sin is that which God has not chosen, but has rejected." It should not be given the honour of being called existent.

Barth's Doctrine of Election

The absolute sovereignty of God (as the presupposition of Barth's whole theology), the *Triumph of Grace* (the title of Berkouwer's book on Barth), comes close to a universalism of salvation. Barth and his followers were always tainted with universalism. The technical term is *apokatastasis panton*. The word *apokatastasis* is found once in the New Testament—in Acts 3:21. It can be translated "restitution" or "restoration." In the context of the Acts passage it means the realization of all prophecy. It occurs in a sermon by Peter in which he challenges all who listen to accept Christ as saviour. But Barth draws this phrase into his peculiar doctrine of election. In Christ, Barth says, every human being is already saved. Christ is the only one who, for our sakes, is both elected and rejected by God. He is the only one who is judged. Everyone is elected, saved, justified, even sanctified, and even called. Therefore the salvation of all is already a fact, only not everyone knows this yet. They need to be told. Conversion here becomes an intellectual step, not

Karl Barth (1886–1968)

a regeneration and a moral conversion: people only need to know what they already are.

Karl Barth of course rejected the accusation that he was a universalist. He stopped one foot short of the gate of universalism. He denies that the devil is the last candidate for reconciliation. But the accusation, once lodged, isn't removed by mere denials.

Barth's Emphasis on the Transcendence of God

Barth's emphasis on God's primacy was a protest against liberalism's domestication of God. But Barth removes the things of God so far into transcendence that his theology is just as much a submission to the dictates of the Enlightenment as liberalism was. A purely transcendent God disturbs secular man's autonomy no more than the domesticated God of liberalism.

There is another problem with Barth's transcendentalization of the gospel. The most potent criticism of religion in modern times, the Feuerbach, Marx, and Freud "projection theory," is also an analogy theory: God is the analogy of man. Barth affirms that the reverse is true, that the primary reality is God. He rejects Feuerbach. Indeed, in the 1920s, he wrote an essay thanking Feuerbach for doing his job for him, cutting down the liberals (who indeed projected from man to God). Barth thought that true theology, his theology, was safe from Feuerbach's criticism because it began with God. But Barth is vulnerable: his reversal of the analogy is based on an unproven assertion.

We will reach solid ground, beyond the Marxist-Feuerbachian criticism of religion, once we leave the exclusive realm of analogies and base ourselves on fact, on reality, on incarnation, on history. History, not Platonizing transcendental theology, is the true touchstone of Christ-ianty's truth. In some ways, a Platonizing theology like Barth's unwittingly verifies the Marxist analysis that theology is only a sub-phenomenon of the philosophy of idealism. So emphasis needs to be put on incarnation, not on transcendence. This is not to say that the Christian faith consists merely in the acknowledgment of historical facts. Then faith would be the same as knowledge. But it is to say that the Christian faith is based on historical facts. Our faith in the Sonship of Christ is based on his words and deeds (*semeia kai terata*). Our faith, for instance, in Christ's resurrection is based on the fact of the empty tomb and the resurrection appearances. In sum, faith is always related to facts plus their interpretation. It is not merely facts, nor is it only interpretation and philosophy. So, in criticism of the middle Barth, the Barth of the analogy principle, it must be said that we need to go back to history as the true touchstone of the Christian faith's truth.

THE FINAL QUEST FOR BALANCE

We have discussed the Barth of dialectical theology, which was the Barth of *diastasis*, of antithesis between God and man. We have looked also at Barth's second great period, marked out by the principle of analogy, and by the writing of the main body of his *Church Dogmatics*. We now move into a third period of Karl Barth's life.

Karl Barth's Self-Criticism in Old Age

As an old man, St. Augustine wrote his *Retractions*, in which he renounced and corrected a number of things he had written earlier. He did not wish to stand before the judgment throne with those things on his account. Something of the same thing happened with Barth in his later years. In 1956, Barth published a little book of fifty pages called *The Humanity of God*. It speaks both of God's philanthropy and his condescension—his coming down—in Christ. This book signals Barth's self-criticism

Karl Barth (1886–1968)

of his earlier dichotomy and diastasis. All our suspicions about Barth are confirmed by Barth himself. Finally, now, he adds the principle of incarnation and condescension to that of analogy. The principle is no longer *katalogia* but *katabasis* (a coming down, not just a thinking down). He adds act to being. From now on, the emphasis is on Christmas, on the incarnation. Barth finally became aware of the danger of dialectical theology: that the majesty of God could be interpreted as the irrelevance of man. That would be a very neat justification of the autonomy of man, of man's secularism. That's exactly what his earlier friend, Gogarten, proceeded to do. Barth now said that what he and his colleagues preached in the 1920s was not untrue, but only half of the truth. He called the previous theology a half-moon theology.

The Holy Spirit as Synthesis

This new departure also has consequences for Barth's debate with Bultmann and the whole subjectivism of the Bultmann school. Barth had been very objective. Man in his theology did not play any role. All was of God and in God. Barth denounced experience and the existential element of Christianity. That had to produce a reaction, which came in the 1940s in Bultmann's school, reducing the whole gospel to an experience of the individual, to seeing oneself in a new light. Barth late in life tried to provide a synthesis between his earlier objectivism and Bultmann's subjectivity. He finds the synthesis in a doctrine of the Holy Spirit. The Holy Spirit subjectifies the objective. The Holy Spirit is the realizer of the gospel. The Holy Spirit brings the majestic God, the transcendent God, into the human heart. Theology is not only about God (as Barth had said in the 1920s), neither is it only about man (as Bultmann said): no, theology is about the communion of God and man in Christ and through the Holy Spirit.

The New Departure Seen in the Church Dogmatics

This more balanced view, which also represents a strong return to Scripture, is announced in *The Humanity of God*, but it can also be witnessed in the *Church Dogmatics*. Around 1955–1956 there is a rupture in the *Church Dogmatics*. The most dramatic rupture is in Barth's doctrine of sanctification. The chapter begins in the old Platonic style, with the statement that our sanctification is only like eddies in the stream, but the last subsection of that chapter speaks about the honour and praise of good works. Suddenly, sanctification is not a matter of looking up and seeing the sanctification of Christ, but of doing good works here on earth, a return to the reality of God's work in history. In the *Church Dogmatics IV/3*, we see the new Barth. He returns to reality.

Barth says, in self-criticism of his earlier image, that God's work of salvation is not some colourful soap bubble which only, like a tangent intersecting a line, touches man on his head. Rather, God's work is not only real in the life of an individual but has also changed history: God's work is actually evident in history (a thought Barth fled from screaming in earlier years). He quotes approvingly the title of the Canadian historian John Wesley Bready, *England Before and After Wesley: The Evangelical Revival and Social Reform*—a work of social history, showing the enormous change in England as a result of the Wesleyan revival movement. After God acts, change can be substantiated. In some ways, Barth returns to an analogy from his first four years before he fell into the bog of dialectical theology: "I can judge from the waves spreading in the pond that a stone of considerable weight must have come down into it." Compared with the enormous repercussions in the Roman empire, the gospel of Christ must have been a mighty factor.

Karl Barth (1886–1968)

The Return of Personal Experience

All this means, suddenly, the return of the importance of personal experience, which Barth had denounced and denigrated. Now, he warns against pure orthodoxy. There is no witness possible (and witness is the essential nature of the Christian) without a personal experience of Christ and the gospel. Personal experience is not the content of the proclamation, Barth warns the evangelical, but no one can truly proclaim the gospel without having experienced it personally. The dialectical theologians' battle cry was "Christ for us." They deprecated any pietistic idea of Christ in us. But Barth, having re-read Calvin's *Institutes*, now says that "Christ in me" is just as important as "Christ for us."

As a natural result of this, Barth reverses his previous criticism of evangelicals. He tells a parable which brings out the necessity of experience. There was a little African boy, he says, who grew up playing with a wooden toy lion. He got used to that toy lion and lived comfortably with it. But he was shaken to the bones when he first encountered the real thing, the roaring lion in the wild. Barth says that's an image for the theologian. Theologians' wooden toy lions are often nice, neat systems of theology, play-things: then one day the real thing comes upon them.

Something must have happened to Barth. The biography makes no mention of it—Barth here makes good his claim that experience should not be the content of one's preaching. But some new experience—an encounter with the roaring lion—must have happened. In the great gothic cathedrals, sometimes the architects put a little picture or statuette of themselves in some hidden place, perhaps the foot of a door. Art historians know that this is the face of the architect, inconspicuous amid the majestic work done for God's glory. Barth's story of the lion must be like that: a modest self-portrait, almost hidden amidst the vast and breathtaking edifice of his theology.

Causes of the Turnaround

So there is a formidable turnaround in Barth, but it has as yet had very little effect in modern theology. Few people recognize it. The question is: what triggered this enormous turnaround? There are three things: (1) re-reading Calvin's *Institutes*, especially that enormous chapter which emphasizes the indwelling Christ; (2) re-reading Bonhoeffer's *Cost of Discipleship* (at the particular point of rupture in the chapter in *Church Dogmatics IV/2* on sanctification, there is a short report on Bonhoeffer's book which marks the change; in preparation for writing the chapter, Barth must have re-read *Cost of Discipleship* and been shaken in his boots when he realized that Bonhoeffer may have been describing the dialectical theologians when he spoke of cheap grace; it would fit the facts exactly, and Barth may have seen himself mirrored here—it must have been an enormous shock: perhaps the roaring lion); and (3) re-reading of Scripture. There are half-a-dozen or more places where he says, "If we want to be true to Scripture, we will have to say . . . ," or, "If we allow Scripture to speak, it would be the case that . . . ." Sometimes the style is such that it sounds as if Barth is arguing with his former comrades.

So at age 70, Barth returned to the reality of God. What are the implications here? Would Barth's recovery of reality and history not require the redoing of his concept of revelation, where the doctrine of revelation is seen, not only as God's decree, but in terms of revelation in history (the kind of effects seen in Wesley's England)? And if it is true that one cannot witness to the gospel without a personal experience of it, then perhaps all those passages which came so close to a theory of universal redemption would need to be redrafted. If all these new things are true, the whole concept of universalism is groundless and rootless.

Karl Barth (1886–1968)

THE BARTHIAN SCHOOL

Simply said, Karl Barth is the greatest theologian of the century. He spawned a large following. A number of prominent theologians, both Lutheran and Calvinist Reformed, form the Barthian school, some of which are still alive. The Lutherans include Ernst Wolf (a church historian), Hans Iwand (deceased), Helmut Gollwitzer (Berlin, prominent in politics). The Reformed include Otto Weber (deceased; his two-volume *Foundation of Dogmatics* was published in 1984) and Thomas F. Torrance (Edinburgh; now retired). Jürgen Moltmann and Eberhard Jüngel, two of the top figures in systematic theology in Germany today, are debatably Barthians. Jüngel is probably the most prominent figure in theology in Germany presently, with his six-hundred page doctrine of God, *God as the Mystery of the World*. In some ways both Moltmann and Jüngel are Barth's grandchildren. Moltmann once declared that he was finished with Karl Barth, that he no longer had any patience with him. Then he enumerated his own teachers who he felt were far more adequate: they were all Barthians. What, then, does it mean for Moltmann to say he is finished with Barth? It is almost impossible to envision him without Karl Barth. The same is true for Jüngel. Jüngel has worked extensively on Barth, but he is trying to be a pupil of both Barth and Bultmann. Jüngel is the one to watch. He wants to combine the two polarities of Barth and Bultmann.

Today, there is still a pocket of Barthians at one university, Göttingen. Hans Kraus, for example, whose handbook of dogmatics is centred on the kingdom of God, is Barthian. But he has recently retired. One of the younger Barthians is Bertold Klappert, though he is not well-known outside of Germany yet. Klappert is another example of a committed evangelical becoming, due to a lack of evangelical theology, a Barthian during his university studies. What does it mean to be a Barthian today? What periods of Barth's life continue to be effective?

Fideism

Characteristic of a Barthian today is the rejection of all natural theology, all religion, and all apologetics: to embrace Barth's "fideism," his approach to theology exclusively through faith and apart from natural theology. It may once have looked brave to refuse to do natural theology, but there's nothing noteworthy about that in our own generation, which leaves no room for God in nature. Few any more are searching for God in nature or in history. So Barthianism is in our time a massive acquiescence to culture: it doesn't disturb culture's sleep but only reinforces our culture's belief that God is nowhere to be seen.

Antinomianism

A second element characteristic of a Barthian today is the slight slant toward antinomianism. This is often an overblown interpretation of Barth's *Gospel and Law*. Barth's pupils are frequently more antinomian than their teacher. Barth's book is itself a fairly balanced statement. He retains some law. But in some of his pupils, the emphasis is gospel, gospel, and gospel.

The Barth of the 1920s and 1930s, the Barth of dialectical theology, has had the lasting influence. Of course, the whole school was formed at that time. Most of the names that we have mentioned picked up from the Barth in the 20s and 30s. Rare is the Barthian who is oriented toward Barth's late phase. Barth's self-criticism regarding the reality of God, of experience, of history, is largely ignored by his pupils. So the final and most promising phase of Barth's life—the one most closely linked to a biblical theology—has had no effect yet, no influence.

Karl Barth (1886–1968)

The Christocracy Concept in Social Ethics

The third thing which remains from Karl Barth (from a period later than the 1920s) is his political ethics. Here Barth's Christocracy is prominent. It is not the ten commandments or any natural law which are relevant to the state's legislation. Rather, the idea is for the state to be modeled after the heavenly Jerusalem. The state should submit to Christ (not God). As always, students get a rough copy of the original stance of the teacher. At times, Karl Barth seemed to have leftist leanings politically. But his letters show that he was far more balanced than the public was aware of in terms of his relationships to leftist organizations. His pupils, though, are usually less moderate. Some are radical leftists, either anarchists or pro-Communists. In Germany today, there is the strange phenomenon of liberal theology linked with a conservative politics, while what used to be orthodoxy is linked with left-wing politics.

BARTH AND EVANGELICALISM

Barthianism, from 1933 on, swallowed much of the remaining presence of evangelicalism in theology. His radical critique of liberalism provided a breathing space for conservative evangelicals. More importantly, they sided with Barth in his defense of the church against National Socialism. Because of that stance, many evangelicals swung behind him. Part of the reason for the disappearance of an evangelical theology was because they associated with Barthianism.

But it was an uneasy alliance for those evangelicals, because in the 1920s and 1930s Barth was seen to be pouncing on pietism whenever he could. Barth saw evangelicalism as the step-brother of liberalism, and just as evil. We saw how in 1925 he accused the InterVarsity group for their subjectivism and anthropocentricity because of their attempt to live holy lives. Only one man, Eric Schick, valiantly attempted an evangelical counterattack against Barth, saying it wasn't right to completely reject the notion of experience and holiness. Schick was the superintendent of the largest mission agency in Germany and Switzerland, the Basel Mission. He was a German theologian who had to live in Basel (the headquarters of the society). He was one of the few evangelicals who immediately recognized Hitler for what he was in 1933. Some took two years, some took twelve years. Schick saw Hitler clearly from the beginning. It was just as well that he lived in Switzerland. He had absolutely impeccable credentials to criticize Barth, because he shared Barth's insight into the nature of National Socialism. Schick said it was ridiculous to abandon the striving for personal holiness in Christianity and to censor personal experience. That is reactionary. We have to have faith and experience. We have to have justification and sanctification. In 1937, he made these claims at a national pastors' meeting. He was howled down by the Barthian pastorate. The Barthians at that time were not a mild lot to live with. It was an unsuccessful attempt, but sometimes we are reduced to doing things just for the record.

North American Evangelicalism and Barth

In North America, Karl Barth has had a checkered history. There were two phases of reaction. The first phase was a rejection of his theology by evangelicals in North America because they were suspicious that his doctrine of Scripture was not quite orthodox. He seemed to be saying that revelation was not in Scripture but somewhere behind Scripture. Scripture was the witness to revelation. Evangelicalism and orthodoxy tend to a position that says the Bible itself is the revelation. Cornelius van Til of Westminster Seminary in Philadelphia led the attack.

Karl Barth (1886–1968)

More recently, there has been a second phase of the relationship between Barth and North American evangelicals, a positive response after the first wave of utter rejection. Clark Pinnock, now at McMaster, said he thought Karl Barth was the next step forward for us. Donald Bloesch, in Iowa, in his two volume *Essentials of Evangelical Theology*, which claims to be the evangelical handbook of dogmatics, often ends up with Barth's solution to particular problems. InterVarsity published Greg Bolich's Master's thesis *Karl Barth and Evangelicalism*, which lists all evangelicalism's positive responses to Barth (and Bolich himself is very positive). The most recent voice is that of apologist Bernard Ramm. Ramm's *Beyond Fundamentalism* seems to suggest that Barth is the next step forward for evangelicals. Perhaps we're in a phase of an undiscriminating acceptance, just as we had a wholesale rejection before. A better approach would be to examine all and retain the good (1 Thess. 5:21).

There is, finally, a confusion among the many evangelicals who do not read Barth, or fail to read him carefully. Barth often used the word "evangelical," but he meant by it something other than what North American evangelicals mean by it. Barth's *Introduction to Evangelical (Evangelisch) Theology*, a beautiful little book of his last lectures, is marvellous, but in North America it should have been titled *Introduction to Protestant Theology*. Barth would never use the term "Protestant" because it is too narrow. By *evangelisch* he means theology's relationship to the gospel. Otto Weber says the term "evangelical" means "Protestant" in German.

REFLECTIONS ON BARTH

My seminars have on occasion been called the "Karl Barth Appreciation Society." Others have quoted me as saying, "All theology is but a footnote to Karl Barth." But it is not true. I am a lapsed Barthian. I try to "Test everything. Hold on to the good" (1 Thess. 5:21), and I try to become no man's uncritical disciple. The first thing is that a clear acknowledgment of Barth's different phases needs to be made. There is that first phase (not counting his liberal student days), 1916–1921, when he shouted "Let God Be God," and out of that conviction produced the first edition of *Romans*. Then there was the phase of dialectical theology and *Church Dogmatics*, 1922–1955. And finally there was the turnaround after 1955–1956.

Weaknesses

There are a number of errors or weaknesses in Barth's theology that need to be addressed. Evangelicals cannot be reconciled with dialectical theology, with its banishment of Christian experience and Christian commitment, its ridicule of the concern for sanctification, its unreality of God, its excessive transcendentalism, and its theological Platonism. Nor can we accept dialectical theology's fideism, the abolition of apologetics, the yielding to the dictates of the Enlightenment, its flight from reason, and reality. A third problem is dialectical theology's political partisanship with communism. Dialectical theologians have, at times, allowed certain political allegiances to almost precede theological truth. Evangelicals sometimes went to Karl Barth because they didn't have their own spokesmen. If we don't do theology, we won't have theologians. So evangelicals went to Karl Barth, the only orthodox spokesperson on the scene, and asked him to say something loud against Bultmann. He would say something like, "Only if you also speak up against the Americans in Vietnam are you entitled to speak up against Bultmann." Barth made political correctness the ground for doing theology. And among his followers, political allegiance often seems to be more important than theological allegiance.

Karl Barth (1886–1968)

Strengths
But Barth has some notable strengths. The first strength is his recovery, in both faith and doctrine, of God as the central theme and principle in theology: "Let God be God." This was a profound correction of liberalism. His second strength is his praise of Christ. His third strength is the recovery of God's work. This came in Barth's last years; it was his self-correction. In those last volumes, Barth gives us things which are found nowhere else today in theology. It is incomparable. Barth's fourth strength is his compelling charm and kindness. And his erudition. He could have been a full professor in six disciplines. Barth was one of those few men who become world famous several times over in a lifetime. By 1930, he had earned a place in the history books, and then he repeated the accomplishment several times again. He was a genius, but he was also "a man with his contradictions." At times he was something of a theological tyrant: despotic, persecuting weaker colleagues. His theology in the middle years was a theological weed killer which also killed many plants.

The Riddle
There remains a riddle in Karl Barth. For one thing, there was the unbelievable self-confidence of the man, which we ordinarily only encounter in leading politicians. In the preface of the second edition of *Romans*, at a time when Barth was no celebrity, he was already talking like a theological emperor. Or there was his comment to Thurneysen that future students of theology would learn the name of his village, Safewil. Barth often appeared to be pretty pleased with himself. It took enormous self-confidence, too, to write with the broad style which filled his fourteen tomes. Other people would be hushed, thinking they couldn't demand that much attention of fellow believers. But this self-confidence might have been part of the reason for Barth's success.

Clearly his is the theological success story of the twentieth century—and he knew it. In some ways, self-confidence and success go together, even in theology. Barth got people to believe in him by believing in himself. Right to the end, he created pupils. He drew people into his world of thought.

Karl Barth and Our Own Situation

We need people today who commit their lives to the service of God exclusively, not to some "-ism" (like liberalism or fundamentalism or conservatism). People who commit their lives to the service of God exclusively will also have to make God concrete and real. Otherwise, people will immediately identify God with some "-ism." It is unusual to see someone committed to God and nothing else, going not to the right, nor to the left, but straight ahead. This concern to serve God alone is at the heart of what Barth was after (even if it was sometimes identified, even by himself, as Barthianism). Don't commit yourself to some faction in theology, Barth said, but serve God. "Let God be God." That is at the heart of Barth's powerful message in 1933's, *Theological Existence Today!* The cry, "Let God be God," had a prophetic ring. At the same time, it fits with the idea of Barth's later years that the purpose of theology is to elevate God. Theology must be praise, not the defense of a certain dogmatic position. That seems to have been Barth's original intention, his original intuition. The implementation of that in dialectical theology by way of a negative theology (negating creation, negating man) was insufficient, but the intuition was right on target. Here is the key to the real battle of our own generation. We need to take over from Barth this concern for the primacy of God. But we also need to add the concern which he only saw at the beginning and end of his life, the reality of God. That is the key issue in today's generation: the primacy and reality of God. To take refuge in theological Platonism, as Barth did in his middle years, is a renunciation of the reality of God and is another way of paying tribute to secularism. The primacy of God becomes only a theory. What is needed is the primacy of God in reality. The seriousness of the prophetic call, the seriousness of battle—with its bruises and martyrdom—only develops with the claim of the primacy of God here on earth, which is a tremendous challenge to modern man's "dark cave" existence. Both the primacy and the reality of God need to be stressed. To do so would carry us a long way in the re-Christianization of theology, of church, and of culture, so that God's will may be done on earth as it is in heaven.

Meditation
Psalm 119:35

> Direct me in the path of your commands
> for there I find delight.

The phrase "direct me," or "make me walk" is traditionally translated "lead me," so the parallels are:

> He led them by a straight way
> to a city where they could settle. (Ps. 107:7)

> Guide me in your truth and teach me,
> for you are God my Savior,
> and my hope is in you all day long. (Ps. 25:5)

The Septuagint has an interesting translation for "lead me." It uses the word *hodegeo*, which means somebody leading the way. It is the same word used in John 16:13: "But when he, the Spirit of truth, comes, he will guide you into all truth." Psalm 119 also says, "Let me walk in the path of your commandment." It is possible that the Hebrew for path refers to an elevated path. So the picture is of walking on a dam through the swamps, uncertain ground to the right and to the left. This is a perfect description of Christian ethics. The commandments are a channel within which to walk. The swamp of human values lies to the right and to the left, but this is the good path. Yet within that path we still need the guidance of God. Even though we know the path to walk—the commands—we still require God's strength and direction to walk it.

Chapter Six

EMIL BRUNNER (1889–1966)

LIFE, WORKS, AND OVERVIEW

Emil Brunner was born in 1889 in Winterthur, near Zürich, in Switzerland. (He is to be distinguished from another Brunner, Peter Brunner, who spent a lifetime teaching at Heidelberg. Emil Brunner was at Zürich.) Brunner died two years before Karl Barth. He studied in Zürich and was chaplain in a small village in Switzerland, then went to be a teacher in a high school in England. This experience opened his eyes to world Christianity. He's one of those few professors of theology who have actually served in a parish. He was pastor in a rural church (at Obstalden, a mountain village in the Canton of Glarus) from 1916–1923, with a year off as a fellow at Union Theological Seminary (1919–1920). From 1922 he was also a lecturer at Zürich. He was made full professor of theology at age 35 in 1924 and remained there. Only after his retirement (1953–1955) was he professor at the newly founded International Christian University at Tokyo.

There is very little on Brunner's life, as no one has seen fit to write a biography so far, and those who write about him seem to have read very little of his material. Despite his importance, there is no school of Brunnerians to look after the fame of their master.

Brunner was one of those people who could write a book a year. In 1921, he wrote his *Habilitation* (which qualifies one as a university lecturer), *Experience, Knowledge and Faith* (not translated). He had a knack for describing in his title what he was trying to do in his book. His titles are always telling. (Experience is one thing, knowledge is another thing, but faith is *the* thing.) In his first public lecture, *The Limits of Humanity* (1922, not translated), he declared war on liberalism. The year 1924 saw his first major book, *Mysticism and the Word*, a full-scale assault on Schleiermacher, the evil spirit behind all liberalism. He continued the theme in 1925 with *Reformation or Romanticism*. He also in 1925 wrote a popular book, *Our Faith* (translated into 16 languages). From then on he became quite well-known in North America, and his books were translated swiftly. *The Mediator: A Study of the Central Doctrine of the Christian Faith* is a book on the doctrine of Christ, first published in 1927. *Theology of Crisis* (1929) was his first English-language book. It contained the lectures he gave in 1928 at Harvard, Princeton, Hartford Theological Foundation, and Union Theological Seminary in New York. It was Emil Brunner, not Barth, who represented dialectical theology in North America. In 1931 he published *The Philosophy of Religion From the Standpoint of Protestant Theology*.

In 1932 Brunner published the first ethics of dialectical theology, *The Divine Imperative* (a literal translation would be *The* [individual] *Command and the* [general] *Orders*). *Natural Theology* (1934) was his little pamphlet in conversation with Karl Barth, to which Barth answered, *No!* In 1935, there were two little books, one not translated. He was the first of the neo-orthodox to look again into the doctrine of the Holy Spirit. The title of the other book was *The Church and the Oxford Group*. Then in 1937 he

Emil Brunner (1889–1966)

published the most encyclopedic theological anthropology of our century, *Man In Revolt*. There's nothing else which matches its broad approach. *The Divine-Human Encounter* (1938) is on his whole epistemology and is very important in understanding Brunner. It was republished with the proper title as *Truth As Encounter* (1964) with an important additional chapter on the current situation in theology. *Revelation and Reason* (1941) was a full-sized book. *Justice and the Social Order* (1943) was another one-time event, providing a Protestant social ethic. It was the only book in several decades to do that. From 1946 onward, he published his three-volume dogmatics: *Dogmatics I* (1946, God), *Dogmatics II* (1950, creation and redemption), and *Dogmatics III* (1960, faith, the church, and consummation or eschatology). But he had earlier published two chapters of dogmatics as separate investigations, his doctrine of the church in *The Misunderstanding of the Church* (1950) and his eschatology in *Eternal Hope* (1953; the German title is, literally, *The Eternal as Future and Present*).

YEARS OF FORMATION

Beyond Intellectualism in Theology

The period of Brunner's younger years was determined by his quest for ethics and the influence of religious socialism on him. This was the attempt to get beyond intellectualism in theology. (His own godfather was the biographer of Blumhardt [*Jesus is Victor*], bringing Blumhardt's influence into his life and theology.) In 1909, Brunner was a participant in the Christian World Student Conference at Oxford. When he came back, he said that above all he had experienced that Christianity was not only a worldview, but a force of life. When we address ourselves to this phenomenon with cold reason, we miss all the religious and moral stimulation. This can be seen in terms of the three elements in the human mind which Schleiermacher identified: will, feeling, and thinking. Brunner discovered that continental theology was solid on the thinking side but missed out on the "religious," the whole world of the emotions, and it missed out on morality. Brunner saw that clearly and early. His first sermon, given in October 1912, was called, "Your Kingdom Come." He interpreted the kingdom as something not merely eschatological, after our earthly life, but in the sense of, "May your kingdom come to us."

Brunner and Socialism
In those years, Brunner became a pupil of religious socialism. He read fervently Kutter's *They Must*, which said that God was secretly at work in the socialist movement and that the workers must behave as they do, even if they're unruly or atheists. In those early years, Brunner strongly participated in the religious socialist movement and wrote articles. He attacked, for instance, capitalism in general and, in particular, those who made money in the arms race of World War I. He joined the November 1917 Swiss general strike, which was a nasty affair. The militia were called out against the workers, leaving a number dead in Zürich. Brunner said genuine socialism and the gospel are inseparable. This is interesting and ironic, because later in life, especially after World War II, Brunner was the most outspoken anti-Communist of all the German-speaking theologians, and quite outspoken against Barth's leftist leanings.

CO-FOUNDER OF THEOLOGY OF CRISIS

The Primacy of the Theological Question
Of the two fathers of religious socialism in Switzerland—Leonard Ragaz and Hermann Kutter—Kutter was the one with the more theological thrust. As with Barth and

Thurneysen, Kutter became more influential for Brunner. The theological concern in some ways began to take precedence over the social question. Kutter was leading back to theology, saying, "God is the social question."

The task today is to announce God as God again to a new generation (as Barth said in 1916). Before, Kutter had said that the theological question today is to be found in the social movement. Now, twenty years later, he saw it the other way around. What is necessary is to announce God again to a secular society. The theological question is the real question in society. In addition, Kutter bequeathed to Barth and Brunner his thrust, in theology, toward objectivism as opposed to individual experience. Brunner, early on, joined the battle against liberal anthropocentrism in theology.

Brunner's Theme: Experience, Knowledge and Faith

In September 1921 Brunner published his thesis *Experience, Knowledge and Faith*. That title remains the theme of his whole life's work. It says that faith goes beyond the subjectivism of people's experience, which he also calls Romanticism. But faith also goes beyond the objectivism of those people who make God a piece of knowledge (that is, orthodoxy). Experience is too light. Knowledge is also insufficient. Faith is the thing.

Because liberal theology was the rule of the day, Brunner first had to battle Schleiermacherian subjectivism. His first book was written at the same time as Karl Barth's second edition of *Romans*. Brunner's book announced the dawning of a new era in theology, pointing away from Schleiermacher and Ritschl, away from all modern theology with its historical relativism and psychologism, away from "that religion of modern mystics and Romantics and kingdom of God pragmatists," and back to God, back to faith. So, against the religious subjectivism dominating the present age, Brunner said that we have to settle the account with Romanticism and pragmatism and establish the objectivity of faith again. Experience and knowledge are only preliminary half-truths. The respective movements—orthodoxy, pietism and evangelicalism—are only half-truths. It is time now for pure objectivity. The consequence of the traditional emphasis of orthodoxy on the objectivity of doctrine is so important that even the ethical is secondary. If the doctrine is clear, and believed, then ethics is secondary. That approach is characteristic for dialectical theology, as we have seen. As with Barth, Brunner's thesis is scathing. Another angry young man jumped out on the theological stage, with fire in the bones. It is astounding that the theological faculty accepted his thesis. Most professors would have sent him to a popular publisher, but few would acknowledge what he had done as a piece of research. It was a manifesto. *Reformation or Romanticism* is similar.

The Dialectic of Experience and Objectivity
The destruction of the archenemy Schleiermacher came in Brunner's four-hundred-page *Mysticism and the Word*. Brunner sets up an antithesis between, on the one hand, the modern form of religion, which really is a form of subjectivism (Brunner calls it "mysticism"), and, on the other hand, Christian faith. Schleiermacher is the great exponent of Romanticism and subjectivism—of "mysticism." The battle between mysticism and faith must be decided. On the title page, Brunner has two mottoes: from Goethe's drama *Faust* which describes the Romantic mood, "Feeling surely is all. Names are but noise and smoke." That quotation actually comes in the context of someone asking, "Do you believe in God?" The character answers, "What do you mean, 'God?' God is a name." Feeling is decisive, not the name. Names are smoke and noise. Goethe had exactly rendered the gist of Schleiermacher's *Speeches On Religion*. Schleiermacher had suggested that it is not important whether you have a

Emil Brunner (1889–1966)

personal or an impersonal God, only that you have strong religious feelings.

That's one side. On the other side Brunner had a quotation from Martin Luther, *verbum est principium primum*, "the Word is the first principle." Feelings are tertiary. Brunner calls mysticism "the other religion" which is sucking up Christianity, posing as a higher form of Christianity. Mysticism always seeks the darkness of feeling and silence. But God spoke and there was light. We must choose either mysticism and experience or the objectivity of faith. Experience is no longer a necessary half-truth but is now an either-or.

"Mysticism"

As briefly mentioned above, Brunner calls religious subjectivism "mysticism." These young theologians in their early thirties had strong convictions, but lacked corresponding historical understanding. A trenchant critic might say that they themselves were exponents of subjectivism: they had more convictions than material. Brunner, for example, fails to make any basic distinction between the pantheistic type of medieval mysticism and a biblical mysticism which remains in humility under God and disciplined by Scripture. Johann Tauler (c. 1300–1361) was a mystic but had nothing to do with pantheism. On the other hand people such as Pseudo-Dionysius and Meister Eckhardt (c. 1260–1327) were pantheistic mystics. Barth also affirms things thunderously which he really knows nothing about. Say something loudly enough, and people are impressed and don't ask any questions. Brunner's unfortunate use of the word "mysticism" when he means subjectivism has no quality of a historical distinction. It is just a weapon, a tool of denunciation, a piece of rhetoric.

At any rate, Brunner pointed out that Schleiermacher was the most important and dangerous representative of this modern philosophy of immanence which takes more interest in the "how" of faith than in the "what" of faith, and more interest in man than in God. That's a good observation, because the followers of Schleiermacher to the present day are very interested, for instance, in hermeneutics. The importance of hermeneutics for the Bultmannians takes over theology. The medium, or the theory of the medium, is the message. We haven't outgrown that yet. Brunner wanted to shake off this evil heritage and come back to truly do "theo-logy," to speak about the Word of God, and not some "anthropo-sophy." *The Mediator* (1927) was an attempt to salvage Christology after the plunderings of liberal theology.

Emil Brunner was one of the foremost representatives of the "theology of crisis," dialectical theology. As such he was invited to present the new movement in Europe and the United States. He had a very successful lecture tour in 1928 and published the lectures as *Theology of Crisis*. The first chapter—worth the price of the book—is a description of the desperate state of theology in Brunner's own time. It is an eerie chapter to read: it is as though Brunner wrote it yesterday. The whole Barthian and Brunnerian theology, it turns out, has been an intermezzo. We're back to the original situation of liberalism.

FINDING THE OTHER SIDE OF THE MOON

Reality in Christology

Karl Barth spoke about "half-moon theology" in 1955. Emil Brunner had a similar experience, only much earlier. It was a rediscovery of the earthly realities of anthropology and ethics. It is good to reaffirm the divinity of God, and keep God and man apart (as in dialectical theology), instead of mixing them up in a theology of immanence. But isn't Christian faith primarily about the reconciliation between

Emil Brunner (1889–1966)

God and man? Isn't Christianity really a story about a relationship between the two parties? God cannot be only a negation of man, so that when God is proved right, man must be proved wrong. Why should Christ be *The Mediator* (1927) if man is not really an entity that can be mediated? Before the 1920s were out, Brunner regained an awareness of the relationality of theology.

The Other Task of Theology: Apologetics

Brunner's search found its first expression in a hermeneutical format. In 1929, he published an important essay, "The Other Task of Theology" in *Between the Times*. That other task was apologetics. Emil Brunner said theology must not just proclaim the testimony of revelation vertically from above (in Barth's phrase), but it must show that the basic questions of human existence find their answer in the doctrine of the church. The message must be related to human existence. The message is not like lightning striking a cavity, or a hollow space (another one of Barth's images). Emil Brunner here anticipated the method of "correlation" which we ascribe to Paul Tillich. Human problems are answered by the message of the gospel. This would also mean that faith can be at home not with rationalism, but reason. Instead of the previous proclamation of eternal strife between God and man, Brunner now proclaims the harmony of revelation and reason, and also of revelation and reality. Faith is true realism. Perhaps some of his experiences in England in his younger years now come back to the surface.

He's not realigning himself with liberal theology. Nothing of the kind. But he sees there's more than the hammer of dialectical theology. Apologetics is not the first, but certainly a necessary second task of theology. But this rediscovery is not a form of accommodation, as in liberalism. Rather, we have to understand apologetics as "eristics"—controversy.

"Apologetics," from *apologia*—giving an answer—seems to make it defensive; but that is not the attitude of the gospel at all. Theology must be offensive. It must go on the attack. *Eris*—fight—replaces *apologia*. Theology must destroy the false confidence of rationalist man. It must, before the gospel can be preached and understood, destroy man's fake solutions. Brunner was after the same thing as Francis Schaeffer was in his "pre-evangelism."

The Search for a Point of Contact

Another of Brunner's famous phrases, coined in the essay "The Other Task of Theology," was "point of contact." Emil Brunner was looking for a point of contact. When I studied theology, anybody looking for a "point of contact" was a laughing stock. But Brunner had a concern here. He was not looking for a positive point of contact, something in human nature which can be built on. He was looking for a negative point of contact. This new stance was also provoked by the questions of the thinking lay Christians around him in Zürich. He said the problems of today's world can no longer be ignored. We need a Christian basis for culture. We need to relate to culture. It is a service of love. In other words, it was Brunner's interdisciplinary concern which made his new departure necessary.

An Ethics of Dialectical Theology

As a consequence, in 1932 Brunner wrote the first ethics of the dialectical theology movement, a feat which had been thought to be impossible. Dialectical theology meant that there was such a vast, enormous distance between God and man that whatever happened here in the present darkness, good or evil, didn't make much difference. Ethics was not really necessary. Distinctions were not really possible. But now, Brunner writes an ethics, *The Divine Imperative*, (or literally *The Command and the Orders*). The first part is

Emil Brunner (1889–1966)

an individual ethics, the second part a social ethics. In the individual ethics, Brunner travels—or blazes—completely new paths. The first half of this book is the seminal document for situation ethics in our century. Brunner said that we must not understand God's command as something eternal, an eternal norm.

Brunner, at that point, had no use for the ten commandments. He doesn't even mention the ten commandments in his six-hundred page ethics. God always speaks into the situation. It is always personal, even to the point of excluding any general rule. So it is very much a situational ethic. But when Brunner comes to social ethics, he discusses the need for some commonality of understanding. If everybody receives intuitions vertically from heaven, then living together becomes impossible. So Brunner discovers that there are certain orders which create harmony between divergent individuals. He speaks about family, church, work, and state in the traditional way. And here, in the second half, another new development in Emil Brunner's theological biography occurs: a first reconsideration of the concept of natural law. There are rules in creation itself which we must abide by.

In later years, especially in *Justice and the Social Order*, Brunner consciously addresses the necessity to re-employ the concept of natural law, a disgusting concept for a twentieth-century Protestant theologian. He is the only Protestant theologian to look at this traditional and Reformational concept of doing social ethics. After Kant, no one in Protestant theology wanted to have anything to do with natural theology or natural law. So in *The Divine Imperative*, Brunner is sitting on the fence. The book is a snapshot of somebody leaving the house of dialectical theology and going back to more traditional paths of theology (just as Karl Barth did in his return to neo-orthodoxy, only in a different fashion).

This same return to questions of real life prompted Brunner's 1934 book on natural theology, *Nature and Grace* (the old scholastic formula). He was now on a collision course with Karl Barth. In line with "The Other Task of Theology," Brunner looks not only at natural law, but at the whole question of natural theology. He suggested that we must go back to see how much validity there is in natural theology, how much of the image of God remains in man. But he raised the question at the most unfortunate possible historical moment. At that moment in history, National Socialism had a strong influence on Christian sympathizers. The question for German Christians was, "Is there any other source of divine revelation besides Christ?" Traditionally, natural theology had said God also speaks through nature and history. So the German Christians answered, "Yes, God does reveal himself in history." And they tended to see Hitler as God's rescuer for the downtrodden German people.

Barth, in stark opposition to this, had, since 1931 and his book on Anselm, been doing away with all natural theology. In 1934, he even had it resolved by a national synod at Barmen that there should be no other voice except the voice of Jesus Christ. That was when Emil Brunner wrote. When the heat was greatest, he dared step into the fire. Brunner said in his preface that he felt he had been mistakenly identified as a traitor to the cause of dialectical theology, even as a "liberal neo-Protestant" who wants to mediate culture and the gospel and return to culture-Christianity. Brunner wrote, "Karl Barth reminds me of a brave soldier on night watch shooting at anyone who doesn't give the watchword, and sometimes even shooting at a friend whom he, in his diligence, hasn't quite understood properly." We know what Karl Barth's answer was. He didn't shoot; he ordered a canon.

Emil Brunner's thesis was that natural theology was true insofar as the image of God remained in man even after the fall. Brunner denied that the image was present in a substantial sense, as if there were remnants of righteousness. But the image of God in man remains in a formal sense. That formal sense is his answerability, his responsibility. Thus, there is a revelation of God in nature. However, it can only be properly interpreted and understood from the standpoint of faith in Christ. Still, there is a point of contact in man.

So, Brunner asserts, there is a natural revelation, but not a natural theology. That distinction is very important. It is an injustice to Emil Brunner to say that he wanted to do natural theology. He says that natural theology is impossible, but there is a divine revelation in nature, seen only by the light of the gospel of Christ. Brunner argued that we need this point of contact for both hermeneutics and ethics, because we have to find common ground with non-Christians if we are to sustain life; that common ground is possible only on the basis of natural revelation.

Brunner simply had a different circle of problems in mind than Barth. When he said we need to have a common basis with others in order to sustain life, he didn't have the National Socialists in mind. He was thinking of the people who were struggling with the effects of the 1929 crash. He was thinking of the Christian economists and lawyers that he was surrounded with in Switzerland. He simply had a different set of problems before him than Karl Barth had in the church in Germany. And that is why the two clashed.

ANOTHER ATTEMPT TO RETURN TO REALITY: THE REALITY OF SANCTIFICATION

In the years 1935–1936, Brunner made the Holy Spirit and the fruits of faith a special topic. "But the fruit of the Spirit," Galatians 5:22 says, "is love, joy, peace, patience, kindness, goodness, faithfulness, gentleness, and self-control." Is that a reality or something only to be believed? Is the fruit of the Spirit something that only God knows we have, something to which we possess the title but not the experience? The primary emphasis of dialectical theology, we saw, was the imperceptibility of God's work in the world: Platonism, God's complete otherness. In Brunner's first book, in fact, he denounced experience. What triggered this new turn? In 1932, Brunner had a personal encounter with the Oxford Group, a sweeping movement of the Spirit. It called for a change in people, not only in their hearts but in their relationships with other people and things. They used as a basis for self-evaluation and repentance Christ's four absolute moral standards (derived from the Sermon on the Mount): absolute honesty, absolute purity, absolute unselfishness, and absolute love. To accomplish this required a commitment to live under the guidance of the Holy Spirit.

Pneumatology and Sanctification

In theological language, the Oxford Group marked a new advent of pneumatology. It was new in that it was an ethical, not an aesthetical, pneumatology: it was about doing good, not feeling good. Emil Brunner encountered this movement, not just as a theory, but as a sweeping movement of the Spirit. There were changed lives all around him in Zürich. People to whom he'd tried in vain to convey the Christian message were suddenly changed and willing to pray and fight alongside him for the Christian message. Brunner became aware of a concrete experience of the Holy Spirit—he described the Holy Spirit as the orphan of Protestant theology—and aware, too, of the reality of God's work of sanctification: sanctification was a living experience, not just a private conviction. Brunner began to think that the doctrine of sanctification and the doctrine of the Holy Spirit had been lost together.

Emil Brunner (1889–1966)

Excursus on the Doctrine of the Holy Spirit

There is a tragic history in the church concerning the Holy Spirit. It began in the early church in the battles against Montanism and gnosticism. These movements emphasized the Holy Spirit, but they turned away from biblical doctrine. In the battle against these very powerful and dangerous heresies, the church struggled to emphasize ecclesiastical offices and authority, in contrast to the uncertainty, the unpredictability, of the free Spirit. As early, then, as the second and third centuries, there was a loss of balance between Spirit and ecclesiastical authority. In theology and doctrine, from that point, only the *person* of the Holy Spirit was taught. The doctrine of the *work* of the Holy Spirit disappeared.

This is another example of dynamic biblical thinking being replaced with static Greek thought. This is true not only of early theology, but also of Protestant orthodoxy after the Reformation. In Protestant orthodoxy, the doctrine of the Holy Spirit is only a sub-topic under the doctrine of the Trinity.

So the second major tragic step in the history of the doctrine of the Holy Spirit occurred in Reformation times. The Protestant Reformation was an anti-charismatic movement. The Spirit was ousted. The spiritualists of the sixteenth century had thrown away Scripture because they felt they had the inner light of the Holy Spirit, which produced a violent reaction in the magisterial Reformation. Due to the influence of German mysticism, Luther was initially very open to the concerns of Christian spirituality. But some wildfire, some "prophets" came through Wittenberg in 1522, travelling from Zwickau in eastern Germany, and Luther saw it as anarchy. From then on, Luther reacted violently. The decisive year was probably 1525, the year of the Peasant War. But up until the middle years of the Reformation, there was, in both language and content, a great openness to the doctrine of the Spirit among the reformers. The anticharismatic years were the post-Reformational years, years of retrenchment and fortification.

Calvin followed a similar trend. In Calvin, all the language of the doctrine of the work and person of the Holy Spirit is present. He emphasizes the Holy Spirit, bringing in, on any pretext, the Spirit's work. The Holy Spirit, however, always points back to Scripture. What does the Spirit do himself? He is reduced to the one who motivates. He is the motivation to do the good, but he is not the instructor about what the good is. He gives power but not direction.

Passages in the writings of the spiritualists give reason for this kind of reaction. Juan de Valdés (c. 1500–1541), for example, a Spanish mystic of that period, compares Scripture to a portrait and the Spirit to the presence of Christ himself. But if we can have Christ's presence, what need have we of the portrait? Or Valdés says Scripture is like a burning candle while the presence of the Holy Spirit in our heart, Christ's presence in our heart, is like the sun. But who will use a candle when he has the sun? Valdés asks, "Does this mean we throw away the candle?" No, of course we don't. Why? It may be of good use to others. Yet Valdés implies that he himself has the inner light and so no longer needs Scripture.

It is this sort of thing which made the magisterial Reformation legitimately react against spiritualism. This kind of spirituality opens the door to complete subjectivism. If Scripture is no longer the standard, then all kinds of things can happen, and did. The Müntzerites, with one man taking twenty or thirty wives, are a glaring example. Against that, the Reformers taught that the Holy Spirit guides, but he does not "guide immediately." He always guides with an intermediate agent, and that is the law, the ten commandments (according to Calvin, as well as the Lutheran 1560 Formula of Concord). The Holy Spirit is reduced to the power, the motivation, for actions already made known through Scripture. The reformers banished the idea of the Holy Spirit as the teacher, which of course is a main concept of Scripture.

There is a third tragic development, and this may have been in the back of Brunner's mind. It is the twentieth-century clash of a new spiritualist movement with orthodoxy. In the revival movement of 1905–1906 in Germany there were evangelistic mass meetings held in Kassel with an evangelist from North America. He brought two girls from Norway who were presented as Spirit-filled media. They prophesied, and there was speaking in tongues. These tent meetings got so out of hand that the official sponsors called in the police to shut the place down. It was a very traumatic experience for German evangelicalism. Since then, there has been a deep rift between evangelicals and pentecostals in Germany. The evangelicals in Germany hold a view that is very similar to the North American Baptists—they are rather suspicious of all pentecostals.

Karl Barth and Emil Brunner had originally, and explicitly, denied the visibility of the works of God in the reformation and transformation of a person. Sanctification was only an imputed judgment of God. Then Emil Brunner wondered if the lack of visible fruit in the Christian church, even the discouragement of a search for real fruit, was possibly related to the loss of the doctrine of the Holy Spirit. Since then, Emil Brunner has been associated with the quest for the reality of change in Christian conversion. So, in 1935, he gave three lectures in Copenhagen on the work of the Holy Spirit and, in 1936, he wrote a little book, *The Church and the Oxford Group*, where he emphasized genuine newness of life, not only in the book of heaven, but in human experience.

A THEOLOGY OF PERSONALISM

How do we recover the doctrine of the Holy Spirit in a proper balance with Scripture? And how do we recover the reality of sanctification in the Christian life? In Emil Brunner's pursuit of a theology which combined the objectivity of orthodoxy and subjectivity of experience, he developed a theology of personalism. *Truth As Encounter* (1938, 1964) is decisive for this. Having battled Schleiermacher and experience, now years later he turned against the hardening of Christian truth into orthodoxy. He declared that faith is not the mere acknowledgment of a certain number of doctrinal statements proposed to the believer by the church, not just a matter of acceptance of propositions. By now, Brunner understood that doctrinal orthodoxy always neglected ethics, always ousted the Holy Spirit whenever he stirred. Through Brunner's experience with the Oxford Group, he also saw that the rigidity of orthodoxy was not just the phenomenon of seventeenth-century theology but present in Karl Barth's own neo-orthodoxy. There is all the anxiety for pure doctrine, but no care about people. And there's no interest in the realization, the implementation, of God's truth of salvation in the earthly life of people. There is, for sure, a danger of mere subjectivism. But there is also the danger of mere objectivism. Objectivism makes God unreal, never meeting the concrete needs of people.

Faith as a Relationship

Brunner tried to strike the balance between objectivism and subjectivism, and found a methodological answer for doing so in the philosophical anthropology of two previous writers who at that time were still fairly unknown. One was an obscure Austrian primary school teacher, Ferdinand Ebner, who taught in a remote village all his life and only wrote one book, *The I and the Spiritual Realities*. That was the germ of this whole development, which was then picked up by the famous Jewish philosopher Martin Buber. The central idea here is the "I-Thou" relationship. True humanity cannot be found in an "I" as such, an individual person, but true humanity can only be found in an I-Thou relationship, in a human relationship, in a relationship in general. (Buber's Old Testament heritage is obviously coming through in this. Greek thought is expressed always in terms of individual existence.) This means we have to distinguish an I-Thou relationship (relating to personally) and an I-It relationship (relating functionally). Faith—and this is the crux of the theology of personalism—is not an I-It relationship but an I-Thou relationship. Faith is a living relationship, involving trust and confidence, and is not just giving assent to some body of doctrine. Faith can also not be an I-I relationship. Faith is not, as some people want to have it, a relationship to the self, which is what Ludwig Feuerbach said about Christianity.

Truth as Encounter was republished in 1964 with an extensive addition. In his brilliant, terse way, Brunner sketches the contemporary theological situation, giving a shrewd, short overview of the modern history of theology up to the mid 1960s. Brunner, in 1964, saw the book as still exactly on target, because that era faced a system of objectivism on one hand (Karl Barth) and subjectivism on the other (Rudolf Bultmann) and both were—and remain—insufficient. The Christian faith is a personal relationship: "objective" and "subjective" are not suitable categories—not wide enough and deep enough to contain the richness of living faith.

Brunner's Dogmatics: *God's Acts in History*

The fruit of Brunner's new epistemology was his three-volume *Dogmatics* which followed, beginning in 1946. Brunner's new departure, marked first by *Truth as*

Encounter, is also clearly evident in *Dogmatics I* on his doctrine of God. His methodological discovery allowed him to produce the long-overdue critique of the traditional doctrine of God which always speaks in terms of God's static attributes, using an ontological form of theology. Brunner returned to a dynamic view of God: God seen through his acts in history. This new approach derives from his vision of truth as encounter. Brunner tries to liberate dogmatics from Greek thought forms and to recover biblical thinking for theology.

In detail, Brunner was the first to come up with a blasting critique of Pseudo-Dionysius the Aeropagite. Pseudo-Dionysius was the sixth-century neo-Platonist philosopher who posed as a disciple of Paul and so was received as a fundamental authority in the medieval church; he poisoned the whole history of theology with his neo-Platonism. Debunking Pseudo-Dionysius is not just a matter of correcting the history of doctrine; it is, in fact, decisive in the light of the Marxist-Feuerbachian critique of Christianity. Marx and Engels' critique of religion was based on Ludwig Feuerbach's critique. Feuerbach attacks those forms of Christian theology that had been developed on the basis of Pseudo-Dionysius, with his ontological statements of God's essence and attributes: God is omnipotent, omniscient, etc. Pseudo-Dionysius makes no reference to the actual history of God's works on earth. His is a philosophical theology. And that falls victim to the Feuerbachian method of criticism, because without any historical rootage, the theology is unsupportable, vulnerable, flimsy. Feuerbach reduces all philosophical speculations about God to man simply projecting upward, unto "God," enlargements of human nature: man has power, God has all power; and so on. This is the "projection theory" of religion.

Brunner removes theology from the threat of Feuerbach by emphasizing the history of the work of God. Interestingly,

Emil Brunner (1889–1966)

Feuerbach knew his weakness at this point. He was sensitive to the fact that he had mounted a valid criticism of ontological theology, but also that a historical theology would create the whole problem anew for him. To this, he had no answer.

Marx and Engels criticized their mentor Feuerbach because he had not provided the tools for a historical critique of Christianity. Since then, the whole history of the criticism of religion in Marxism has been an unsuccessful attempt to furnish the additional historical critique. There was one attempt of which Karl Marx was particularly proud. It described Christianity as a distant development of the Old Testament Molech cult, where the son died for the father and at the hand of the father. So they said Christianity was only a spiritualized version of the ancient cult. Of course, in the Molech cult the victim was burnt and not crucified, but that didn't bother them. Ironically, the inventor of that theory converted to Roman Catholicism five years later and renounced everything he had written. So dust has covered those books and the Marxists are still trying to find a natural genesis of Christianity.

THE MISUNDERSTANDING OF THE CHURCH: THE CHURCH AS A FREE ASSOCIATION OF BELIEVERS

We've seen Brunner's attempt to bring the objective and subjective together in faith and to recover the reality of the work of the Holy Spirit. In 1950, he brought this program to bear in his book on the doctrine of the church, *The Misunderstanding of the Church*. In some ways, the book is a restatement of the age-old theory that there is an antithesis of the Spirit and the institution.

Brunner's hypothesis is that for eighteen hundred years the church has been caught up in a terrible misunderstanding. The misunderstanding consists in the identification of the *ekklesia*, by which Brunner means the free community of Spirit-filled followers of Christ, with the church as institution. That, he says, is mistaken objectivist thinking. The church has become a bureaucracy, an institution, not a personal fellowship. The church began as a fellowship with no institution, a fellowship of communion with God and one's brethren. But, Brunner says, look at what we've done with it—look, for example, at the Augsburg Confession, the basic document of the Protestant Reformation: there, the true marks of the church are reduced to pure doctrine and proper administration of the sacraments. Taken to extremes, that approach could make the pure church no more than one preacher and one listener. Church becomes an activity for Sunday morning. But that is not the New Testament concept of the church. Brunner saw that the contemporary church lacked inspiration, which was the hallmark of the early church. Church order and church law had become surrogates of real life. Theology, finding that it could not establish command over the paralogical effects of the Spirit, therefore mistrusted the Spirit. And so historically, the *ekklesia* very quickly turned into an institution. Brunner thinks he can see that decay already in the pastoral epistles with the establishment of offices; he therefore argues that the pastoral epistles must be late (second century), and not from Paul.

Spirit Versus Institution

Brunner recovers an earlier notion of the incompatibility of the New Testament, the Holy Spirit, and the institution of the church. This was originally stated by Rudolf Sohm, a church lawyer from Harnack's generation. He was the first to say that there is a basic incompatibility between Spirit and institution. He added that there is no hope that they can ever be reconciled, but that what has happened is necessary. Law is always incompatible with the free flow of fellowship.

Emil Brunner (1889–1966)

Harnack, in his famous *History of Doctrine*, makes the same point. The development of the second century was the "churchification" or the "dogmatization" of the original uprising of the Spirit. Christ brought the kingdom of God, and what developed was the church.

As a result, the Spirit was everywhere excluded. The degeneration was completed in the established church of the Constantinian age. The pinnacle of institutionalization was the canonical law of the Roman Catholic church. That was the crust that hardened over everything. And the Reformation was only half-hearted with respect to the antithesis of law and Spirit. They did not break with the institutional church.

But, Brunner says, the *ekklesia*, this free-flowing fellowship, cannot be suppressed. Whenever church becomes an institutional giant, the *ekklesia* emerges in the form of "heresies." In some ways, it is like a strip of land left uncultivated at the far end of a garden. All kinds of migrants begin to camp there. That far end of the garden is the doctrine of the Holy Spirit. If we don't take it under cultivation, the migrants will pitch their tents there.

Brunner says that the *ekklesia* has always been there in some hidden sect. In the twentieth century, it is to be found mainly outside of the organized churches. Brunner says he has personally seen it in two groups: the Oxford Group and in the Non-church Movement of Japan.

What is to be done then? Shall we destroy the existing structures? No, we must change the direction of development. We must not stress "churchiness" any longer but must take the existing churches as the vehicles or vessels of the Spirit, not closing him in any more. Brunner admits that the institutions have proven useful at least for the tradition of Scripture. If we had had *ekklesia*—this free-flowing fellowship—it is doubtful that we would have had Scripture after twenty centuries. Suddenly, at the end of

Brunner's book, he sees that there might have been some good in the institution. What we must do today is create living cells, Christian communities. The same is true of the ecumenical movement. It is ridiculous to think that an organizational unity would bring any progress. It must happen locally.

The book met with a roar of disapproval. At the time, everybody shook their heads over Emil Brunner. He was a bit too early. Later on, Karl Barth made a similar revolutionary step away from infant baptism, a move which also undermines the institutional church. Nobody shook their heads at Karl Barth; then, they simply got scared.

A Critique

There are weaknesses in Brunner's interpretation of the Scriptures. The antithesis of institutionalized church and *ekklesia* is, in fact, not present in the New Testament. We find church structure and even the initial forms of church legislation in the indisputably genuine epistles of Paul. Paul says this is what we have decided and that is what is taught in all the churches (for example, in 1 Cor. 11:16). There is a binding rule from the apostle and it is not left to the individual local congregation to make up their own mind as the Spirit directs. In the New Testament, there is a harmony of law and Spirit, not the antithesis the Brunner wants to see.

The precariousness of Brunner's solution can also be seen in the house church movement in Japan. When he was in Japan, the movement was in its heyday. But, it has often been observed, strong house churches tended to die when the leader died. The non-church movement purposely has no organization as a church. The only organizational link is a magazine. The groups are autonomous, and once the leaders are gone, there is no structure to hold them together.

Emil Brunner (1889–1966)

It is typical of Brunner's style that, out of an initial and revolutionary vision, he launches out with fierce polemic, cutting right and left, throwing stones at everybody who is in the way. Then, even before he has reached his goal, he begins to withdraw some of his contentions. *The Misunderstanding of the Church* fits this pattern. He cannot sustain the fierceness of his attack to the end of the book. By the late chapters, he's already redressing the whole argument. Brunner does that frequently. It is as though he's giving his publisher a chapter at a time so there's no way to correct earlier material.

BEYOND WRONG

Alternatives in Eschatology

In 1953, Brunner published *Eternal Hope* (a literal translation would be *The Eternal as Future and Present*). The battle between a present and a future understanding of eschatology has been with us since the beginning of modern theology. The present day understanding of the eschatological can be found as early as Schleiermacher. At the end of his second speech in *On Religion* (1799), he wrote, "In the midst of finitude to be one with the Infinite and in every moment (now) to be eternal is the (true) immortality of religion." That is the modernist understanding of eschatology—it is prominent in Bultmann—where the doctrine of the "last things," *eschatos*, is not understood in terms of time, but in terms of final and utmost significance for our present life. It is understood in a qualitative, not a temporal, sense.

Yet the New Testament contains both ideas of eschatology, even in the same document (for example, in John's gospel). Clearly, the resurrection of the dead is a topic of eschatology. In John 5:25, Jesus says, "I tell you the truth, a time is coming and has now come when the dead will hear the voice of the Son of God and those who hear will live." That is what Bultmann emphasizes. But there is also an expectation of a future resurrection: "Do not be amazed at this, for a time is coming when all who are in their graves will hear his voice and come out—those who have done good will rise to live, and those who have done evil will rise to be condemned" (Jn. 5:28–29). So John has both understandings of eschatology, the present and the future, experience and expectation. As is often the case in the New Testament, truth is found in paradox, in tension. It is not usually possible to say that Matthew has one particular view and the author of Revelation has another. Rather, the different views exist side by side. Quite often biblical truth is two times one hundred percent: it is modernist rationalization which tears them asunder. When that happens, the roots for two opposing schools in theology have been created. The same dichotomy was seen with the idea of the kingdom of God in Ritschl and his son-in-law Johannes Weiss. Ritschl had a completely present day understanding of the kingdom of God, but Weiss said that in the New Testament it is strictly future. Biblically, it's both.

In the 1920s, dialectical theology held, collectively, a present-day understanding of eschatology. It was pioneered by Paul Althaus (the Luther expert) who in *The Last Things* (1923) reintroduced present-day eschatology. Eschatology is not something in the future, but in transcendence. You live each moment with reference to eternity. There is a vertical line upward from each moment of our lives. This is an existentialist concept of eschatology, what Barth called in *Romans* the "infinite qualitative difference of time and eternity." Or when Bultmann describes Jesus's teaching, it is always "the last hour." Everyone followed Paul Althaus in this. But in 1945, Althaus publicly renounced his earlier position and returned to a future eschatology.

Emil Brunner (1889–1966)

It is in this war theatre, in this context, that Emil Brunner comes up with a formula that is closest to Scripture. He said eschatology is not either/or, but both/and. With reference to Romans 8:11, he says, "The life of the believer is the experience of resurrection, and an expectation of resurrection." He thinks that is also true in the larger framework, in that we speak of the *parousia*, the presence of Christ. He has come, he is now with us, and he will come in glory. In addition, Brunner emphasized not merely the objective reality of the *parousia* but also our subjective involvement in it. As always in his teaching, Brunner tries to combine the objective and the subjective.

A CRITIQUE OF EMIL BRUNNER

Negative Aspects

J. Edward Humphrey, one of Brunner's most penetrating critics, is correct in desiring more certainty from Brunner with regard to the Holy Spirit's inspiration of Scripture. Humphrey observes that Brunner is prepared to make courageous statements about creation and revelation. Why not a similar courage about the inspiration and preservation of Scripture? It is a bit eerie, Humphrey says, to see how arbitrary Brunner sometimes is about what is really "biblical" in Scripture and what is not, as if he had an ulterior standard to decide what's genuine. An example is his denial of the virgin birth. Brunner's argument is that the virgin birth is only in Luke and in Matthew. But the Lord's Prayer is also only in Luke and in Matthew. Creation *ex nihilo* is also only found in a few places in the Bible. Does it go, too? Brunner's is a remarkably rationalist position. Indeed, there are a number of places were Brunner suddenly looks just like a liberal.

There is also some uncertainty in Brunner's eschatology. Brunner stresses the fundamental importance of human responsibility. Responsibility is Brunner's major anthropological category. And yet he hesitates to accept the particular doctrine from which the whole concept of responsibility is derived, the concept of a last judgment. Like Karl Barth, Brunner is reluctant to exclude the idea of universal salvation.

Positive Aspects

Brunner's style is always clear, concise, crisp. He is not baroque like Barth. Brunner wants to be immediately understandable. He writes for the educated Christian, the lay person, but also for pastors. He is not content with inner theological rhapsodies, but has one of the strongest interdisciplinary concerns of modern theologians. Theology is part of the service of the good Samaritan: it must be applicable. Brunner was quite successful with this approach and, in his time, became very influential among professionals—lawyers, politicians, sociologists. But that may have meant that he was less influential among theologians in the church. Emil Brunner lived first in the shadow of Karl Barth, and later in the shadow of Bultmann. Not infrequently, in his dogmatics and in his ethics, he said what Barth said, only twenty years before Barth. In other areas where he stood apart from Barth—such as in his idea of natural revelation—he was attacked unjustly. Often he was attacked and then proved right in the event. Brunner often measured himself by Barth and was hurt by the comparison. Even his acknowledgment of Barth's exploits express this sense of competition. On the other hand, Brunner is highly innovative. But he is not very strict in his argument; he is often fuzzy and sometimes even self-contradictory. He pontificated and made harsh judgments, but then a few pages later was forced to withdraw half of what he said. He was a man, like all theologians, with his contradictions. But he's worth studying again, especially

Emil Brunner (1889–1966)

his books of the 1930s and early 1940s when he came into his own, when his strongly innovative spirit was most in evidence.

Perhaps Brunner's remaining traces of liberalism, the denial of the virgin birth, and his tendency toward antinomianism (1932 and later), cost him his greatness. In the long run, and seen from sufficient distance, rationalism is always mediocre. But overall, Emil Brunner stands, after the interlude of dialectical theology, for a great quest: the recovery of the reality of God.

Meditation
PSALM 119:45

And I will walk about in freedom,
for I have sought out your precepts.

This is a most striking verse, a paradox. The Lutheran translation has, "I will walk joyfully for I seek your precepts." That's something in itself: that God's ordinances should be a source of joy in your walk. But far more paradoxical is, "I shall walk in liberty." The old English Catholic translation has, "I will walk at large"—I will have plenty of space, as I walk the road of your precepts. It is a part of our whole western tradition that the law is perceived as something hedging in the individual. There is no concept of the law of God giving you freedom. The twentieth century thinks freedom is lawlessness. The Old Testament has a completely different mindset. Freedom and law go together.

Grammatically, the law is the presupposition of freedom. Clearly there are other bonds in life, other than the divine commandments, which one might choose. If you pursue what you think to be freedom, you might find yourself no longer at liberty. You have bound yourself by the repercussions of your deeds. You were at one point free, but no longer. You might have avoided the consequences if you had looked at the commandments of God, which, after all, are the owner's manual for life.

Chapter Seven

RUDOLF BULTMANN (1884–1976)

LIFE AND WORKS

Bultmann was born in 1884 (within five years of Barth and Brunner) and died, almost completely blind, at age 92 in 1976. He was one of those theologians—their number is legion—who was never a church pastor, being just a New Testament scholar.

In 1912, Bultmann was made an assistant professor of New Testament at Marburg. He was a full professor at Breslau and Giessen. Then, in 1921, he returned to Marburg and was there until his retirement in 1951. Marburg is a small university town in the heart of Germany. From 1928, he came under the influence of the existentialist philosopher Martin Heidegger. In 1933, he was one of the few professors who took a clear stand against National Socialism, although he did it in a way that did not rob him of his chair (as in the case of Barth).

Major Works

In 1921, Bultmann came out with a very important book which has changed the face of New Testament scholarship: *History of the Synoptic Tradition*. It made him a co-founder, with Karl Ludwig Schmidt and Martin Dibelius, of

Formgeschichte, form criticism. Form criticism is the study of the development of the materials in the synoptic gospels in terms of their particular forms and genres. There is an attempt to distinguish between the Jesus material and the legend created by the early church. There is a distinction here between the tradition and the redaction, for example, to discover what Matthew added to the same story in Mark or in Luke. Form critics want to discover the personality of the author and his "theology."

In 1926, Bultmann published *Jesus and the Word*. For the first time, we see what is decisive in Bultmann: his strong systematizing hand, ranking him among the last two centuries' prominent systematic theologians. Bultmann was philosophically educated, and so naturally developed a system of theology. *Jesus and the Word* presents a very existentialist Jesus and, before Emil Brunner, a full-fledged program of situation ethics. Jesus is the enemy of the law. The believer is autonomous.

The year 1933 saw the beginning of the publication of Bultmann's volumes of essays. The first is *Faith and Understanding*, which includes a number of famous essays. The second volume came almost twenty years later, in 1952, *Essays Philosophical and Theological*. The third volume came in 1963, and the fourth volume in 1965.

The Gospel of John: A Commentary (1941) was revolutionary on a number of levels. Even more revolutionary was "New Testament and Mythology," a lecture given in a small hidden village in the Black Forest in 1941, right in the middle of the war years. The lecture was republished ten years later and spread like wildfire. It created the Bultmann school and established his reign of dominance. This essay outlined the program of demythologization. It is found today in the book *Kerygma and Myth*, which also has a number of responses from prominent theologians, and other essays by Bultmann in response to those responses.

Rudolf Bultmann (1884–1976)

A few other titles are important. In 1949, Bultmann published *Primitive Christianity in Its Contemporary Setting*. In 1948 and 1953, he published his *Theology of the New Testament*. In 1956, he published a volume of his university sermons, *This World and Beyond*. He gave the 1955 Gifford Lectures (published in 1957), *History and Eschatology: The Presence of Eternity*. Finally, in 1958, he wrote *Jesus Christ and Mythology*, published first in English.

ROOTS

Bultmann is firmly rooted, and in a double way, in the tradition of Kantianism. Both the theological and the philosophical faculty at Marburg (where he studied and taught) were neo-Kantians. On the philosophical side were people such as Hermann Cohen (1842–1918) and Paul Natorp (1854–1924). The theological side was all Kantian. Wilhelm Herrmann (1846–1922), Ritschl's pupil, dominated the theological faculty from 1879 to 1917. Herrmann's work was really a prefigurement of existentialist liberalism, which became the formula for Bultmann. Herrmann was also Karl Barth's teacher. Barth departed both from liberalism and existentialism in the direction of objective orthodoxy. But Rudolf Bultmann all his life remained a true pupil of his teacher Wilhelm Herrmann, embracing existentialist liberalism. In the last analysis, Wilhelm Herrmann was a blend of his own two teachers, August Tholuck (pietism) and Albrecht Ritschl (Kantianism). He really is the embodiment of the existentiality of faith versus orthodox teaching.

Even Bultmann's ethics in *Jesus and the Word* (1926) can be traced back to Herrmann. Bultmann's situation ethic, with its personal autonomy, resembles the individualistic ethics of Herrmann, where all of the emphasis lies on personal decision instead of given standards. In both the realm of belief and the realm of living, in both dogmatics and ethics, it is personal decision and personal conviction, not external standards, which matter.

DIALECTICAL THEOLOGY

Rudolf Bultmann set out as one of the closest colleagues of Karl Barth in the 1920s. He made his personal declaration of war against liberalism in 1924 with the essay (also in *Faith and Understanding*), "Liberal Theology and the Most Recent Theological Movement." In this good and trenchant essay he takes Barth's side in the debate against Harnack. He attacks the inner-worldliness of liberal theology and its domestication of the gospel. The gospel, above all, is *skandalon*, scandalous to the human mind. That has been forgotten in liberalism. Bultmann here comes out in the spirit of dialectical theology—theology as a negative word, a word emphasizing the disharmony between God and world. Christianity is other-worldliness, not inner-worldliness. God is the Wholly Other, the utterly transcendent. That means that God represents the crisis of the whole world of man and history. God means the total abrogation of man, his negation. He is—this echoes Barth—the judgment of man.

God's Transcendent Judgment

Bultmann was as far from a concept of incarnation as Barth was at that time. And, parallel to Barth, Bultmann's negative theology affected his understanding of ethics. There can, he declared, be no such thing as a service of God on earth. There can be no work for the kingdom, as the liberals and the pietists say. All human activity is sinful and doesn't fit into the kingdom. God's demands can never be fulfilled on earth.

We glimpse the influence of Kierkegaard here. Bultmann said that the most rotten thing in liberalism was its use of the Sermon on the Mount, as if it were a prescription for living. Rather, the Sermon on the Mount demonstrates the scandal of Christianity because it demands the impossible. Bultmann represents the age-old idea that the Sermon on the Mount only points out human sinfulness. It is not a program for living. Thurneysen, Barth's friend, had called the Sermon on the Mount the "unscalable mountain wall." Bultmann quotes Thurneysen's peak statement on the sinfulness of man: "Because of the sinfulness of man on principle, sin is not a matter of individual moral lapses. A few steps more or less in the wrong direction do not make a difference." That is what the whole of dialectical theology really arrived at: the ontological, not the moral, evilness of man. Man is the enemy of God, not by his rebellion, but by his creation. The only hope, therefore, is faith in God. Justification, again, does not change the quality of a person in this visible world. The new man is only present in God's transcendent judgment, not in our experience. This is to be believed, and must be believed in the face of the visible evidence, which is quite opposite. Here, in Bultmann's very first essay, he makes a basic statement which he held to all his life, the axiom of the invisibility of God and his works. Nothing of God's works are to be seen or experienced.

EXISTENTIALIST LIBERALISM

Bultmann's own stance is that of existentialist liberalism. In 1925, he published his second important essay (also in *Faith and Understanding*), "What Does It Mean to Speak About God?" Here, Bultmann resumes the theology of his deeply Kantian teacher Wilhelm Herrmann, and links up with liberalism again and the whole tradition going back to Schleiermacher. His thesis is that, when speaking of God, we can only say what God does to us. We can make no objective statements about God. Under the presuppositions of Kantianism, in which objective reality is completely usurped by the sciences, the only position left for theology is subjectivity. This is also what Kierkegaard said. All natural theology and any philosophical proofs for the existence of God are phantoms. Nothing can reach the transcendence of God.

Subjectivity as Decisionism

At this juncture, though, Bultmann introduces a distinction from the subjectivity of the nineteenth century. He denies the subjectivity of experience, which is foundational to Schleiermacher and Herrmann. For Bultmann, God is the abolition of all religious experience. Bultmann's subjectivity is, instead, a subjectivity of decision: an ever-renewed decision of faith in the invisible and the transcendent God. This whole stance in Bultmann and his school has been called "decisionism." There is no firm foundation for faith. Faith, rather, is an ever-new decision. So faith is a machine gun experience, a choice repeated staccato-like over and over, which makes it highly subjective.

Existentialism and the New Testament

In the essay "What Does it Mean to Speak about God?" Bultmann also says that nothing changes in our life after conversion. The absolute transcendence of God is and remains Bultmann's primary principle (as in Schleiermacher). Since we are continually sinful, we are continually being justified. This divorce between who we are and how we live was what made Brunner so nervous in the 1930s. In 1928, Bultmann wrote another famous essay, "The Meaning of Dialectical Theology for New Testament Scholarship." This essay forms the link between his early subjectivism and the mature stance of the program of demythologization. Here Bultmann argues that the biblical text is not a source for objective historical truth or events, but rather speaks in the

Rudolf Bultmann (1884–1976)

present because it speaks of my existence (this is almost verbatim Schleiermacher). We must, therefore, have an existential interpretation of Scripture, not just a historical recounting. But by "existential interpretation," Bultmann does not mean personal interpretation, an interpretation in terms of the individual. Instead, he means an interpretation in terms of man. Bultmann uses "existential" in anthropological terms. The theme of the New Testament, he says, is existence, not history.

Existentialist Subjectivity

The Bultmannians are all strong on hermeneutics, language being everything for them. They make sophisticated semantic distinctions between, for example, one type of history and another. They distinguish *Geschichte* (the Anglo-Saxon word for "something which has happened") and *Historie* (the Latin word for "history"; the adjective is *historisch*). This distinction is difficult to translate into English because we only have one word for "history." They also make a distinction between *existential* (a technical term which came with the philosophy of existentialism, a term of philosophical and theological anthropology, denoting general conditions of human existence and the predicament of humanity as such—in Heidegger it is even used as a noun: death, soul, fear are existentials) and *existentiell* (something that is of uttermost importance to me: not just a state of mind, but something which changes my life, striking at the heart of my existence). Bultmann's language almost echoed that of some rural pietistic grandfather who hungered for the sermon to be *existentiell*, to change the lives of people, not just give them some food for thought. Existential, in contrast, means an interpretation of Scripture, not in personal terms, but in terms of human nature and human existence. So Bultmann's subjectivism is not to be understood in the old sense of the nineteenth century.

Bultmann and the Older Liberalism

There is another difference between Bultmann's liberalism and the nineteenth-century brand. The older liberalism had described certain stories in the New Testament as non-historic, and so winnowed them out. Bultmann's approach is not elimination, but reinterpretation. The New Testament must be reinterpreted in the deeper sense of human self-understanding. The legendary material wasn't to be eliminated, only interpreted so that its meaning for human life might be discovered.

THE FULLY DEVELOPED POSITION

Bultmann's mature position is his program of demythologization and existential interpretation. The program is described in his famous essay, "New Testament and Mythology" (1941). The presupposition for Bultmann's program is the straight acknowledgment of the victory of the Enlightenment as spelled out since Kant. Bultmann, then, is one of the most prominent Kantians in modern theology.

This presupposition, which he expresses in very clear terms, is the clash between the scientific world view and the "mythical" world view of Scripture. The scientific world view contends that we are living in a closed universe. And within that universe everything is governed by two laws: analogicity and causality. This means, of course, that, by definition, nothing totally new can come in.

Bultmann tries to accommodate himself to that closed universe with the theory of the absolute transcendence of God: God is absolutely beyond. However, what he calls the "mythical" worldview, the worldview of Christianity and perhaps other religions, speaks of the entry of God or of gods into this world. It speaks of events and effects that break through Kant's iron curtain between transcendence

Rudolf Bultmann (1884–1976)

and immanence. Bultmann defines the story of God's coming down here on earth as a myth. In the clash of these two worldviews, the scientific worldview and the mythical worldview (which has a sort of perforated universe where divine influences come into this world), Bultmann takes for granted that the scientific worldview is victorious.

Therefore, he argues, we have to do away with a literal understanding of things such as the incarnation (God coming down to become man), bodily resurrection (something which has no analogy), ascension (another perforation of the iron curtain), and the visible return of Christ. We can no longer understand these in a literal sense. They don't make sense within our scientific worldview.

Bultmann, in pursuit of his program, tries to make allies of the New Testament writers. He argues that the reinterpretation of biblical stories may be in harmony with the secret intention of the gospel itself. The gospel writers never want to make statements about physical causes and effects in the past. Rather, they want to touch us personally in the present moment. Faith is believing, not seeing. This spells the end of all objectivism. The world of objects is the property of science.

Demythologization and the existential reinterpretation of the gospel, Bultmann claims, is an application of Martin Luther's famous phrase, "faith alone and not by works." It is an application of that statement in epistemology, the field of the theory of knowledge. By faith alone, and not by seeing, do we know God. Bultmann takes the cardinal principle of the Reformation doctrine of salvation and transfers it to epistemology—by faith alone, and not by facts.

So Bultmann's program is to first demythologize, in order to, second, reinterpret existentially. That is necessary, he says, because all myths really express existential, anthropological truths. They may on the surface describe some isolated past event, but behind that surface they really describe the human predicament: fear, anxiety, death, life, growth, joy, pain—the existentials of which the philosopher Heidegger had spoken.

Examples of Demythologization

As an example, let's take the existential reinterpretation of the biblical miracles. One famous story which has been popular in the Bultmann school is the story of Jesus calming the storm (Matt. 8:23–27 and parallels). Bultmann says that story is an expansion of the existential truth that the church is a tiny little ship tossed about in the turbulent sea of the unruly world of nations. The sea is an Old Testament image for the world of nations. So the church is always threatened with submersion. But in the moment of greatest danger, it finds itself preserved by the (of course) invisible presence of Christ. It is an existential truth of danger and salvation expressed, perhaps for the simple-minded, in story form. In some ways, Bultmann's view of New Testament religion is comparable to Hegel's definition of religion: religion speaks about something in the form of imagination, in pictures, which philosophy treats through language and logic. Religion pictures truth, philosophy defines it.

Bultmann speaks similarly of the bodily resurrection of Christ. It is not an event in the past but an existential truth. He thinks 1 Corinthians 15 is a fatal and unwelcome kind of argument by Paul. The Easter event, in contrast to Paul's or anyone else's insistence on its historical facticity, is the faith of the disciples of Jesus: in spite of Christ's crucifixion, they still believed, they still had confidence in the power of his eternal words to live beyond his death. The stubborn faith of Christ's disciples—not the fact of Christ's resurrection—is the Easter event. Resurrection was their interpretation, the meaning they gave to the cross. Similarly, today's proclamation of the gospel, the re-presentation of the story of Jesus, is to been seen as the event of salvation. There's

Rudolf Bultmann (1884–1976)

a surprising parallel here to the philosophy of the Roman Catholic mass, that this moment is the saving event. When the Protestant preacher preaches the gospel, that is the saving act. The disciples witnessed to the continuing power of the earthly personality and message of Christ in their own proclamation. Jesus, according to this view, is risen again in the preaching of the church. The church's preaching is Jesus' resurrection life.

A third example of this demythologization and existential reinterpretation is Bultmann's famous demythologization of the Holy Spirit. Bultmann builds his argument on the principle of contrast. This is evident in the structure of the first eleven lines of his essay on this topic, with its quick succession of contrasts: "certainly . . . but . . ."; "true . . . yet . . ."; "even . . . but . . . ." What is Bultmann contrasting? The first thing is Paul's own belief with the popular belief of his day. Paul is, to begin, culturally bound in his statement that the Spirit manifests itself in miracles and as an agent in extraordinary psychic phenomena. Paul simply embraces the culture's popular belief at this point. But Paul becomes aware of the questionable nature of that popular view in his discussion with the Corinthians. Clearly, he sees, the popular view of the Spirit as an agent needs to be shed. Of course, Paul regards the Spirit as a "mysterious entity," and he speaks of the Spirit as a kind of "supernatural material." That's what comes out if Paul is read "literally." But here Bultmann introduces the antithesis. "In the last resort . . . ," Bultmann claims, Paul really means something else. By "Spirit," he clearly means the "possibility of a new life." Paul describes the Holy Spirit, not in terms of works, but in terms of possibility: not agency, but ontology.

That's Bultmann's first move. His second it to claim that the Spirit's possibility must be "appropriated by a deliberate resolve." In the demythologized view, in other words, the decisive action belongs to the human agent. The New

Testament portrays the Holy Spirit as the divine subject of action. But Bultmann, in his existentialized format, says that human action, or human decision, is decisive. We have moved from theology to anthropology, from dogmatics (speaking about God's work) to ethics (speaking about man's actions), from actuality to possibility. That is the nature of demythologization. By a trick of interpretation, all that's left of the original biblical concept is an empty shell of language. The content of that language has been fundamentally changed, from God to man, from the work of God to the action of man. So demythologization is, at root, a transformation from a theocentric gospel into an anthropocentric ethics. The gospel declares what God is doing through the Holy Spirit; Bultmann speaks about what man must do.

Bultmann's silent presupposition is that the biblical histories are myths. He doesn't argue that; he just accepts it. The Random House dictionary defines "myth" as a legendary story, usually concerned with deities or demigods, and with the creation of the world, and as a belief which is accepted uncritically. That's the general definition of "myth" current in our language. But for Bultmann, "myth" has a highly specific meaning. Myths are all those stories which speak about divine action entering into this world's reality, transcendence breaking through into immanence. In short, everything which violates the Kantian iron curtain is "myth." Those myths must be demythologized. So before the actual process of demythologizing begins, a presupposition has been made: stories of transcendence into immanence are myths. But this is presupposed, not argued.

Bultmann's silent presupposition is that biblical history is really mythology. This is important to note: demythologization is also de-historification, turning history into myth.

Rudolf Bultmann (1884–1976)

The most surprising result at this point is that Bultmann has done exactly what Feuerbach did to religion. Feuerbach also took statements which predicated something about God, timeless "is" sentences of a religious philosophical kind, and then de-theologized them, turning them into anthropological sentences. But before Feuerbach could do that he had to silently shift Scripture's historical statements into timeless "is" statements. This tactic is clearly seen in Feuerbach's *The Essence of Christianity* (1841), where he takes the sentence, "God created man after his image," which describes a concrete action and makes a historical claim, and silently, subtly turns it into "man is the image of God." The statement is no longer about an act, but rather describes a timeless quality. After this, Feuerbach turns the sentence around and says, "No, God is the image of man." It is that turning around which comprises the reduction of theology to anthropology. But beneath this is a secret, uncontrolled presupposition: an event, an act of God in history, has been turned into a timeless sentence.

Only those timeless sentences can be converted into anthropological sentences. A historical event can't be turned around. The irony here is that Bultmann's theological demythologization parallels the method of the man who was one of the most prominent nineteenth-century atheists.

BULTMANN AFTER DEMYTHOLOGIZATION

Bultmann holds the view that Christianity is other-worldliness. It has nothing to do with the world of objects. Christian faith, rather, is a new self-understanding. This is an interesting formula. The only object of "understanding" is the "self": "understanding" is the predicate, "self" the object. That, of course, is the perfect solution to the threat to Christianity from the objective reality of science. Faith, simply, is to see oneself in a new light. You remain the same person; you only understand yourself differently. So nothing takes place which might contradict the claims of physics or biology or psychology or history. In a manner reminiscent of Schleiermacher's discussion of the virgin birth, Bultmann says an act of God always occurs in an event which is completely natural and which can only be seen as an act of God by a person with eyes of faith. Faith, then, is a different interpretation of reality. Reality remains the same, but faith interprets it differently. This is what Feuerbach always criticized. Feuerbach said Christians have an eye disease. They see things that are not there. Bultmann in some ways supplies the proof for the accusation.

Bultmann, in the essay in which he responds to his critics in *Kerygma and Myth*, gives his worldview in a nutshell. At the beginning, there is the undisputed presupposition, the axiom, of the invisibility of God. This axiom excludes every "myth" which tries to make God and his acts visible. Both the visibility of God and the visibility of his acts are ruled out in one sweep.

Therefore, we believe in God in defiance of all outward appearance, against the evidence. There is no evidence for God or for the works of God. We simply believe. Bultmann later writes, "You must plunge into the inner darkness." This language betrays him, for it is the language of medieval mysticism. Bultmann's theology is a new version of the old mystical theology of negation. Nothing can be seen, nothing can be ascertained. Just believe. As in justification, so in epistemology, we must believe against the evidence. On the one hand, good works are ruled out; on the other, ascertainable knowledge is ruled out as well.

What is true for faith is also true for ethics. Bultmann attacks sanctification. We must, he says, think of everything as profane. We must believe, again contrary to the evidence, that God is Lord of everything. Bultmann says that here lies the perfect solution to the demands of secularism: simply accommodate it.

Christians must be the first to acknowledge the secularity of the secular. But Christians then believe that, in spite of the visibility of the secular, God is the master of the universe. It is a naked belief. "The framework of nature and history (both) is profane, and it is only in the light of the word of proclamation that nature and history become for the believer, contrary to all appearance, the field of the divine activity." In itself, the objective world is black. But for the believer, once he hears the proclamation, it becomes white. The world changes its nature for the eye of the believer who beholds it. It "becomes" for the believer. Again, faith is interpretation of reality. "It is faith which makes the world profane and restores to it its proper autonomy as the field of man's labours." This echoes the first speech of Schleiermacher's *On Religion*. Religion here gives back—restores—to the world all those things that had been thrust on it—everything in the field of science and metaphysics, of ethics and politics. Religion gives these back and then withdraws. In Schleiermacher's case, religion withdraws to the emotions; in Bultmann's, to the airy, lofty realm of self-understanding.

Summary of Demythologization

In demythologization, the language of the gospel is preserved, but not its original content. That must be reinterpreted. The rolled-away stone of the Easter story, the cross of Christ—all must be reinterpreted. In the same way, Bultmann retains faith in the forgiveness of sins but dispenses with Christ's vicarious suffering—Christ representing us—as the objective basis for forgiveness. Where does forgiveness then come from? From God. We cannot say more than that. God is the bare principle of the causation behind everything (as in Schleiermacher). So

Bultmann has little interest in anything historical, little interest in the history of Christ. His concern, rather, is the meaning of existence, the meaning of human life. This is why hermeneutics takes over from doctrine. In some ways, demythologization is the creation of a new mythology, the mythology of self.

Karl Barth, discussing Bultmann's stance, spoke of a "happy inconsequence" in Bultmann. It is all message and no facts. But Bultmann said there is, in the last analysis, one basic act of God. In his essay "New Testament and Mythology," he says the new life of the believer can be described completely in purely human terms. But the transition, from old to new, cannot be described in such terms. Here, we must speak of God, but not in terms of a historical moment in which the change took place; rather, we speak of a transcendent act of God, a divine interpretation. We do not speak of the "what" of divine intervention, only the "that" of it.

This opens the battle to try to capture this last little foothold of speaking about God. The prospect of a God-less, an a-theistic, religion is near the surface in Bultmann. One of Bultmann's colleagues, Fritz Buri in Basel, and the philosopher Karl Jaspers, argue that Bultmann is inconsistent. His message can be fully understood in terms of anthropology, but still he grasps to retain some sliver of theology. Barth said sarcastically that in Bultmann's great theological strip-tease he graciously left his swimsuit on. At least at one point Bultmann held to the testimony of God. But, as his critics—and many later pupils—were quick to ask, Why?

Demythologization, then, is a de-objectification, a de-historification, and a subjectivist, existential reinterpretation of the gospel. It is typical liberal reductionism, reducing theology to anthropology. As such, it plays into the hands of the atheist critique of religion; it is the worst possible preparation of Christianity for the encounter

Rudolf Bultmann (1884–1976)

with the criticism of religion found in Marx, Feuerbach, and Freud. Bultmann furnishes proof that Christianity is nothing but subjectivity and idealism. As we see in his later radical pupils, he paved the road to atheism.

A CRITIQUE OF BULTMANN

There are some positive aspects in Bultmann's theology. His book *New Testament Theology* is impressive. He makes many insightful observations and statements. The liberal theologians typically have dogmatic prejudices, but often they perceive some aspect of the New Testament more vividly than do orthodox or conservative theologians. Because they have less of a doctrinal bias, they are less anxious to conform Scripture to fit their dogmatics textbook. Sometimes the liberals have a philosophical and historical bias, but that may only appear in other places. Bultmann is like this.

He is critical and selective, but in places he clearly describes things as they are; his exegesis is seldom skewed by dogmatics. But, ironically, there is nothing in his *New Testament Theology* on Jesus or the historical gospel. His focus is all on John, Peter's circle, Paul, and so on. Obviously Jesus and the synoptics have been dropped because Bultmann sees the synoptic gospels as pervaded with Jewish religiosity. So Bultmann's freedom from bias in exegesis is undercut by his philosophical prejudices.

Another of Bultmann's positive qualities, according to some, is his seeming concern for hermeneutics to reach modern man with the gospel. And to some extent he did reach modern man with the gospel because he adapted the gospel to the postulates of reason. In some ways, then, Bultmann is a new edition of Arianism (the heresy of Arius). Arius, because of his alleged missionary passion, also criticized Christology. He sifted out the hard parts from the gospel to make it easier to swallow. So a theologian's passion for missionary outreach is not sufficient ground for praise. We must also ask: What is the brand of Christianity to which we are asking people to convert? And at what cost to the gospel have we made the "gospel" attractive?

We've already spoken of the loss of history in Bultmann's theology. If Christianity has only existential appeal, only the power to explain the human predicament and human potential, then any other religion that produces good existential consequences would have the same right and title to being considered truth. Christianity, severed from it historical roots, is robbed of its uniqueness.

It is of utmost importance—the Bultmann school, in a negative way, makes this clear—to retain the historical element in Christianity. That is the ground upon which faith is anchored. Reason can never reasonably explain the origins of the Christian church without the resurrection. It is nonsense to say that the resurrection is nothing more than the Easter faith of the apostles. It is absurd to claim that the disciples would venture out into the world with burning zeal, enduring imprisonment and beatings, facing and embracing death, if Christ was not risen. Mere faith would not inspire and sustain such a thing. If Christ was not alive, they would have quietly gone back to their jobs in Galilee and nursed the wounds of bitter memory. They would, in fact, have felt betrayed by Jesus of Nazareth, not empowered by him. No. Something happened, something not explained in human terms. Something in history.

The Effects of Bultmann's Rule in the Church

Bultmann has been the most influential theologian for over twenty years. He has formed an entire generation of clergy in Europe. With the church in Europe under the leadership of the Bultmannian school for a generation, its largest accomplishment has been to take away the church's joy and courage. It was clearly his school which alienated the

Christian from Scripture. Having driven a wedge between the church and the Bible, he has robbed the Protestant church, a church that was based on *sola scriptura*, of its identity. The church in Europe today looks like a cut flower in its final stage of wilt.

THE PUPILS OF BULTMANN

Here are some quick snapshots of the theologians Bultmann lured into his camp. Günther Bornkamm, a New Testament exegete, is a mild Bultmannian who taught at Heidelberg until his retirement in the 1980s. Ernst Fuchs (b. 1903), at Marburg, is very influential through his pupils and has written a textbook of Bultmannian hermeneutics. Herbert Braun, the most radical of the Bultmannians, occupied the chair of New Testament at Mainz. Probably the best-known Bultmannian is Ernst Käsemann, at Tübingen until his retirement. He has been widely translated into English. He is famous for a commentary on Romans and two volumes of essays.

After these men there is a second group who is roughly ten years younger. But all of them are now retired. Gerhard Ebeling, who was at Zürich, is the only systematician among these people. There was Willi Marxsen in New Testament at Münster and Philipp Vielhauer at Bonn. Hans Conzelmann at Göttingen is perhaps better known, having written a great work on Acts. Manfred Mezger was a practical theologian at Mainz. Finally, there is only one man among the youngest generation. Günter Klein at Kiel is still teaching.

Many of these people took chairs in theology only later in their lives (after the war and prisoner of war camps). They were given these chairs in the ascendancy of Bultmann's own influence.

Bultmann completely dominated the scene between 1950 and 1970. After the influence of Karl Barth waned,

Bultmann took over. There are two rather well known British Bultmannians. Ronald Gregor Smith was professor of systematic theology at Glasgow and was one of the forerunners of the whole idea of secular Christianity. Almost ten years before Bishop Robinson's *Honest to God*, Smith published *The New Man: Christianity and Man's Coming of Age* (1955). Shortly before his death he doubled up with Bishop Robinson with a book called *Secular Christianity*. He was quite respected because he first introduced to British readers the late thought of Dietrich Bonhoeffer—the *Diaries* and the idea of a religionless Christianity. He also introduced Martin Buber to a theological audience. The other Bultmannian who is still teaching is John Macquarrie at Oxford, also a systematician. The titles of his books give the direction of his thought: *An Existentialist Theology, The Scope of Demythologizing, Studies in Christian Existentialism, God-Talk*. He also is among the authors of a great overview of the nineteenth and twentieth centuries, *The Twentieth Century Religious Thought: The Frontiers of Philosophy and Theology 1900–1980*.

Herbert Braun (b. 1903)

A brief study of Herbert Braun, the most radical of the Bultmannians, will show where the road leads. It has been said earlier that Bultmann was inconsistent in demythologizing not the concept of God itself, but only the acts of God. The concept of God, at least in Western languages, has the connotation of an objective entity outside the world, and therefore would have to be a myth on Bultmann's definition. Herbert Braun, with strange courage, removes that remaining inconsistency, and provides a very straightforward form of Bultmannianism.

Herbert Braun's starting presupposition is, to use Bultmann's phrase, the "acceptance of modern man's worldview." That worldview is defined (again echoing Bultmann)

Rudolf Bultmann (1884–1976)

in terms of a "closed universe": a universe that, on principle, is fully knowable and is ruled by analogicity and the cause-effect law. Within this world, two times two is four. We cannot have "two times two is five" on Sundays. No irrational remnant is permissible, no field of religion where the universe's laws are temporarily suspended. A "miracle," in the sense of a divine agent breaking into the world and interrupting the cause-effect chain, is unacceptable to the modern mind. Braun equates Christianity with other Near Eastern religions. It is just a form of religion with no special status. God can, therefore, no longer be understood as existing independently. He can only be understood as the final cause, the "whence," the "wherefrom," of the peculiarly Christian manner of existence. God is nothing more than the "whence," the "wherefrom," of the human feeling of being both upheld and morally challenged.

Does Braun then, like Bultmann, leave a surviving trace of mythology? Braun says, No. "God" no longer implies the concept of transcendence. Human existence is challenged and upheld by something which nevertheless is inside this world: in the last analysis, my neighbor. "God" is only the name, the title, the abbreviation, for a particular kind of human relationship. "God" is mere nomenclature. This is a significant recurrence of that famous phrase from Schleiermacher: "I can only speak about God in speaking about man." "God" is a sociological and anthropological code-word, a symbol for a certain kind of co-humanity, a certain manner of fellowship. This means, yet again, the reduction of theology to anthropology, and Braun freely confesses that he is doing just that. God is only an attribute of human existence. So Braun reduces Christianity very much as Feuerbach did in the nineteenth century. Even the glorification of human relationships was prefigured in Feuerbach. But Feuerbach at least had the honesty to admit that the result of his efforts was atheism.

Feuerbach knew that he was making a clear departure from Christianity, not implementing the deepest intentions of the New Testament. That was left to the Bultmannians to claim. It is consistent with the direction of this theology that some of the most gifted students of Braun, in the next generation, turned into socialists and nothing else. This is the end of the Bultmann road.

Braun himself is a marvelous, elegant, eloquent writer. His most recent book, *On Jesus* (same title as Bultmann's 1926 work), is written in a very straightforward, positive manner and is therefore quite convincing to young students of theology. Here, he describes Jesus as a very fine and congenial man. But only a man. His godhead is a predicate bestowed on him by the church (picking up Ritschl). Braun is the fulfillment of Bultmann's program to adapt Christianity to the dictates of the Enlightenment. It is so fully adapted that it is no longer theology.

Meditation
Psalm 119:63, 79

I am a friend to all who fear you,
   to all who follow your precepts . . .
May those who fear you turn to me,
   those who understand your statutes.

We are given a two-fold approach. The first calls me to be committed to all those who fear God's commandments. At the same time, those who fear God should turn to me and associate with me and link up with me. It is the important question of your allies in your Christian life, your alliances in your spiritual struggle. One should spend a considerable amount of time just to care for one's colleagues, "strengthening the brethren," beginning with a massive prayer of intercession. Who you work with can be more important than what you work at. You might be detailed to peel potatoes. On the other hand, there's the quest for colleagues in this struggle for Christianity. Hopefully you all have a group of friends or allies with whom you share a purpose and convictions. And hopefully you spend enough time to support them and hope that they support you.

Cultivate those relationships, by letter writing or conversation and prayer. Ask for the Lord's inspiration for what you can do next for this or that person. But there is the other side, looking for allies in the struggle for the re-Christianization of theology and the church. We need those with strong spiritual independence who are also headed in the same direction. There's a need to pass on our convictions to the next generation.

Chapter Eight

CURRENT FIGURES AND ISSUES IN THEOLOGY

THEOLOGIANS

The first major theologian of the second half of the twentieth century is Jürgen Moltmann. Born in 1926, he obtained his doctorate in 1952 and was a pastor. In 1957 he was made associate professor at Göttingen and then in 1963 moved on to a full professorship at Bonn. Now he is at Tübingen, where all the action is (Küng, Stuhlmacher, and Jüngel are there and that's where Käsemann was). Moltmann is a Reformed theologian, a Calvinist. He has a number of books on the history of Reformed theology and showed an early interest in the almost-forgotten doctrine of eschatology (with Bultmann everything turned into present-day eschatology). In the 1950s, Moltmann was doing a history of doctrine in terms of eschatology. The fruit of that ten-year endeavour appeared in 1964 in his book *Theology of Hope*, which became an international best-seller. Triggered by the philosopher Ernst Bloch's (a Jewish Marxist) work, *The Principle of Hope*, Moltmann wrote the corresponding theological eschatology to Bloch's philosophical eschatology. His intention was to recover the eschatological perspective in modern Protestantism which had been lost in Bultmann.

The Bultmannian school used the term "eschatological" but meant by it "existential." Unfortunately, Moltmann does not really overcome that attitude with his book. Hope, while the main principle in his theology, lacks content, and while he has changed from a theology of faith to a theology of hope, his theology remains highly subjective.

In the last days of his life, Karl Barth passed severe judgment on Moltmann's eschatology, saying it was as empty of a true Christian content as Schleiermacher's had been. Nonetheless, Moltmann continued to publish very influential books. In 1972, he published *The Crucified God*, and *The Church in the Power of the Spirit* (which he called a "messianic ecclesiology") in 1975. Since then he's written several other important books, including *The Trinity and the Kingdom of God* (early 1980s). And there are many essays on the side, especially on the topics of eschatology, hope and liberation. In the 1960s, he was the star theologian of the World Council of Churches, and he became a point of reference for the theology of liberation because of his emphasis on the future. His own more radical students have long by-passed him, saying he has the ink of the revolution, but not the gunpowder. Recently, he's written a doctrine of creation which hasn't as yet been translated, *An Ecological Doctrine of Creation*.

Eberhard Jüngel

Eberhard Jüngel is also at Tübingen. He may by now be the brightest light of the younger generation. Born in 1933, he is a pupil of, on the one hand, Karl Barth, and on the other, two Bultmannians: Gerhard Ebeling and Ernst Fuchs. Jüngel is attempting today to combine the heritage of both Bultmann and Karl Barth. He's a magnificent talent and an extremely erudite man. He may be the only one of the modern German theologians who can claim to be as cultivated as people like Harnack once were. Even his doctoral dissertation on Christology caused a splash. In 1965, he produced his first systematic theological book, *God's Being Is In Becoming* (on the doctrine of God in Barth), followed by his first volume of sermons in 1968. In 1972, another famous book came out, *Death and Eternity*. His magnum opus, a 600-page doctrine of God, *God as the Mystery of the World*, was published in 1977. It is erudite to the point of being inaccessible. Other writings include a volume of sermons, and a book with Paul Ricoeur (the famous French-American philosopher), *Metaphor and the Hermeneutic of Religious Language* (1974). Unlike other Bultmannians, Jüngel is strongly committed to the church. He is not one of the free-wheeling intellectuals, so common-place in theological science, who stand aloof from the church. He feels an obligation to it. There are a lot of good things to be said about his theology, but it is unclear whether he remains basically a Bultmannian. For him, the contents of theology are, in the last analysis, language events, not historical ones. His theology has been described as "iridescent," a theology which can change colours.

Wolfhart Pannenberg

The third giant of the triumvirate of the German theologians today is Wolfhart Pannenberg. Born in 1928, he received his PhD in 1953. He comes from a Lutheran background. He became an assistant professor in 1955 and a full professor in 1961 at Mainz University, but has his home now in Munich in Bavaria. He has a completely different theological ancestry from the other theologians we have studied. He does not hail from Barth or Bultmann but is in the line of Gerhard von Rad, the Old Testament scholar (although Pannenberg is a systematician). He wrote his theses on medieval theology. His second thesis was on the principle of analogy in theology, but unfortunately it has never been published. Then he became known as the spokesman of a group of young theologians in Heidelberg (where von Rad was teaching) who were attempting to break away from the domination of the Bultmannian school. Pannenberg, in his little pamphlet *Revelation as History* (1961), was the first to challenge the Bultmannians. He was trying, for instance, to recover the historicity of the resurrection. One of his theses in the book is that we must confidently proclaim the historicity of the resurrection. It is not just something to be believed, or something comprised by the faith of the first apostles, but is an actual historical event.

Unfortunately, that group broke up quickly because they were met with so much hostility. Everybody was after them. The Barthians were after them. The Bultmannians were cut to the heart. Everybody who had accommodated to post-Enlightenment thinking felt stung.

Pannenberg also wrote something on theological anthropology, *What is Man?* (Fortress Press, 1970). In 1964, he published his first big book on Christology, *Jesus: God and Man*. Pannenberg has been outstanding in trying to stay in communication with scientists. In 1976, he published a major statement on the relationship of the theory of science and the theory of theology, *Theology and the Philosophy of Science* (Westminster Press). It is an attempt to rebuild a philosophical theology (which had been rejected by both Barth and Bultmann). His original interest in revelation and history is evident; he says we must take a stand against a mere kerygma theology, a theology of the message. In today's world, we must insist on the verifiability of the message. This cuts across everything that Bultmann and Barth stood for. Seeking to restore a place in science for theology, he mounts a strong debate with positivism and critical rationalism.

In 1985, Pannenberg published a major doctrine of man, *Anthropology in Theological Perspective*. He is well-versed with the North American scene and much translated. He comes closest to being a modern philosophical theologian, recovering much of what had been lost for two generations. But it is questionable whether he has the same loyalty to the church as Jüngel. Pannenberg is impressive as the typical intellectual, but not as a pastor.

MOVEMENTS

God-is-dead Theology

The most important development of the 1960s was the God-is-dead phenomenon, or Christian atheism. It was spearheaded by John A. T. Robinson, a New Testament scholar who at that time was the Bishop of Woolwich in London. Picking up on Tillich, the late Bonhoeffer, and Bultmann, he wrote his best-seller *Honest to God* (1963) in which he proclaimed the end of theism. He described God in Tillichian terms as the "ground of our being." Jesus was not the Son of God but the "man for others." For good measure, he threw in the concept of the New Morality, where all the moral absolutes of Scripture were done away with: only love is prescribed, and it is up to each person to decide what love is. Robinson followed this up with *Christian Morals Today* (1964), *The New Reformation?* (1965), and *Exploration into God* (1965), which is particularly important for his dogmatics. This is his declaration of pantheism, an attempt to draw together man's mystical and secular aspirations.

Then he went back to Cambridge, becoming Canon of King's College in order to do some more thinking. But he proved to be a maverick, and in 1976 he came out with *Can We Trust the New Testament?* In a most revolutionary fashion, he came up with a conservative dating for most of the New Testament, reversing an eighty-year trend in New Testament studies. It didn't mean he was moving back toward theism, but he rendered conservatives a remarkable service. He died in 1983.

In America, the death-of-God theology was represented by William Hamilton, who wrote *The New Essence of Christianity* (1961) and *The Death of God Theology* (1965). Then, a lapsed Barthian, Paul Van Buren, in 1966 published *The Secular Meaning of the Gospel*. Thomas Altizer wrote *The Gospel of Christian Atheism* (1966). Since then, Hamilton and Altizer have given up theology and are teaching in English departments. Gabriel Vahanian has a book on the whole phenomenon, *The Death of God: The Culture of Our Post-Christian Era*. Dorothy Sölle is the German representative. She originated the idea of an atheist Christianity, and made statements such as, "If Christ came today he would come with a sub-machine gun." After five years she discovered that God was not dead, but red. Since then she has headed the Christians for Socialism movement. Finally, there is Harvey Cox, who teaches at Harvard and who contributed importantly to this movement with his book *The Secular City* (1963). In it, he solves the problem of secularism by welcoming it wholeheartedly into Christianity. As disturbing as the death-of-God movement was at the time, it seems to have been just a passing wave, a mere fad.

Process Theology

There are two other important streams of thought which we need to mention. The less serious is process theology. Two names represent it today in North America, John Cobb, Jr. *(A Christian Natural Theology,* 1965, and *Christ in a Pluralistic Age,* 1975) and Schubert Ogden, a former Bultmannian *(The Reality of God,* 1966). This is another school in theology based on a recent influential philosophy. In this case, the seminal idea is from Alfred North Whitehead's *Process and Reality* (London, 1925).

Process theologians are quite good in trying to overcome the static Greek ontological thinking in theology and move on to process. But in some ways, to structure thought in terms of process is to still remain in ontology. Process theology is the dialectic of being in motion, and so can be easily accommodated within the field of ontology. Christianity, in contrast, is not about static thought, and not about process either, but about history, events, acts. If theological thought gets stalled in process, then its god will be impersonal or pantheistic—and the process theologians' god is.

Liberation Theology

A more influential movement, and in need of being taken more seriously in North America, is liberation theology. It probably began with Richard Shaull, a North American teaching in Latin America for many years. In the Church and Society conference of the World Council of Churches in Geneva in 1966, he proclaimed a theology of revolution which soon turned into a theology of liberation. There are two prominent liberal Protestant theologians who became spokesman for liberation theology. The first is Rubem Alves, who wrote *A Theology of Human Hope* (1969) and *Tomorrow's Child* (1972). He has since turned away from liberation theology and now speaks of liberation in terms of the individual and Freudian thought. The other major Protestant author is Hugo Assmann. He entitled his book *Theology for a Nomad Church* (1975). The most famous man in the movement is the Catholic Gustavo Gutiérrez, who gave the movement its name. He wrote *A Theology of Liberation* (1972). On the Protestant side, José Miguez Bonino should also be mentioned. His two books are *Doing Theology in a Revolutionary Situation* (1975) and *Christians and Marxists*. Among North Americans who have spoken in this same fashion is Robert McAffee Brown, *Theology in a New Key: Responding to Liberation Themes* (1978). Two other names are Juan Luis Sugundo, and Orlando Costas (*The Church and its Mission*, 1975), who is the closest to an evangelical in the movement.

THE PROBLEM OF EVANGELICAL THEOLOGY

The first thing in summarizing evangelical theology is to ask, "Just what is evangelical theology? Who represents it?" On the one hand, there are the orthodox Reformed. They are still counted as evangelicals, but they exist in a traditional world by themselves (for example, Louis Berkhof, with his *Systematic Theology* and his pupils). There is not much discussion among them of outside developments. Cornelius Van Til (*Christianity and Barthianism*) and Edward Carnell (*The Theology of Reinhold Niebuhr*) are long dead. In North America, knowledgeable people say evangelical theology stands on one man, Carl Henry (former professor at Eastern Baptist and Fuller Seminary and founding editor of *Christianity Today*). Of course, there is Donald Bloesch and Clark Pinnock, but both of them are young.

Carl Henry is the one man who has really struggled to single-handedly represent an evangelical theological position. He is the only evangelical engaging in discussion with mainstream theological development, from Barth to liberation theology, especially in his six-volume work *God, Revelation, and Authority*. In this, it is obvious that he has read vastly. He was a journalist by trade, and this also comes through. There's an incredible amount of material here. But the flaw is that the development of his own systematic stance is submerged under the flood of critical discussions. This is understandable in an evangelical, who has to work his way up from nothing, first having to acknowledge the other streams, the ongoing work of theology.

But it certainly weakens the impact. Many evangelicals also find Henry too rationalistic, and he is strongly indebted to a Christian Reformed philosopher, Gordon Clark. But evangelicalism in North America needs a bit of theory before it gets going again with its many practical concerns. So Carl Henry's work is a most welcome ingredient for evangelical theology.

The overall problem confronting evangelical theology at this point in time is how to represent Christian thought and teaching in an era which is dominated by secularism and human autonomy. How do we translate gospel to culture, heaven to earth, theology to philosophy, transcendence to immanence? How to do it without being, on the one hand, a mere counter-culture, a cultural ghetto, and on the other hand, culture-Christianity, fully accommodated? The task is to address culture without accommodating the message to culture. That's the problem for evangelical theology.

In the confrontation with today's secular mind-set, which is present both outside and inside church and theology, there are two primary goals. The first concern is the recovery and the representation of the primacy of God. We have to pick up and continue Karl Barth's original impetus and emphasis on the primacy of God, and with it reject accommodation to the Enlightenment—which is at the heart of most liberalism—and reject too the *apotheosis*, the deification, of man, where God becomes a kind of extension of man.

The second fundamental problem for evangelicalism is the recovery of the reality of God. This is where Karl Barth struggled. We've seen how Bultmann completely removed God and his actions from earthly reality, from nature and history, and the early Barth did the same with his Platonism. Barth did, late in his life, return to reality—as an old man he had just begun, for instance, to recover the reality of history; but this is certainly not a major item in his system. That needs to be put back in place. We also need to recover—and this hasn't been tackled at all yet—the reality of nature. We need to pick up these threads of the reality of history and the reality of nature from the late Barth, and go on from here.

The concept of reality is important because it not only determines dogmatics, but also ethics. The reality of the work of God in Christ always corresponds to the reality of the Spirit's work in sanctification. A theology which lacks the concept of the reality of Christ's person and work will also lack a concept of reality in its doctrine of sanctification. How do we recover a biblical ethics for evangelicalism? We must go beyond Barth and Bultmann, beyond their transcendentalization of both Christology and sanctification, to recapture biblical realism.

So these two tasks are before us: the recovery of the primacy of God, and the recovery of the reality of God.

A Word of Hope

It was characteristic of the beginnings of evangelicalism, in the pietist movement on the continent, to hope in a better time to come for the church. They believed that the church would break out of its desert wanderings, and would return once again to spiritual power. The pietists were not pessimists, as many evangelicals today are. We too can share that hope if we embrace again not just a faction or an ecclesiastical party, but the primacy and reality of God. The task today is to make an allegiance not to evangelicalism, but to the Lord himself. The aim must be the re-Christianization of theology and church, to give biblical and theological roots to faith again: that is theology's service to the people of God. And if theology and the church are revived, the benefits will overflow into culture.

This means that theologians need honesty and self-criticism, self-criticism under God's standards. We must also recognize that all theological work is not an end in itself. It must serve a purpose. It must serve the goal of a re-Christianization of theology and the church. It must, in the end and above all, glorify God. Therefore, let us close with a prayer.

> *Dear Lord, we thank you for the challenge that grows out of this study of the theology of the past two centuries. You have led us to take upon ourselves, to feel a responsibility for, the development of this very heart of the life of the church, and we would pray that you would guide us and accompany us as we go out. Make us co-laborers with Jesus for a re-Christianization of theology and of the church: to deepen and give roots to faith, to strengthen the brethren, to feed your sheep, and so also to help humanity, according to the orders that we have been given by you. We do thank you for the commission that you have given us. May we be faithful to it. Amen.*

Meditation
Psalm 119:98–100

> Your commands make me wiser than my enemies,
>   for they are ever with me.
> I have more insight than all my teachers
>   for I meditate on your statutes.
> I have more understanding than the elders,
>   for I obey your precepts.

If you delve into the Word of God, you may find that you are closer to the heart of wisdom than your teachers who are highly educated. I knew a fellow student who had a very solid grasp of biblical knowledge, not only of individual verses but in terms of contents and connections. He had read extensively as a young man. It was astonishing to see how well this stood him in his examinations. Christian theology, after all, is based on Scripture. If you study Scripture, you will be able to hold your own in all kinds of situations.

www.ingramcontent.com/pod-product-compliance
Lightning Source LLC
Chambersburg PA
CBHW032039150426
43194CB00006B/345